SCRIPTURE PRO

Carmen Rojas, autho
Bible Every Day, taug
College of the Holy Sp
runs courses for leaders
in the Philippines.

SCRIPTURE PROMISES

Compiled by
Carmen Rojas

Collins
FOUNT PAPERBACKS

First published in 1988 in the United States of America by Servant Books, Ann Arbor, Michigan.

This edition first published in Great Britain by Fount Paperbacks, London in 1990

Printed and bound in Great Britain by William Collins Sons & Co. Ltd, Glasgow

CONTENTS

Introduction

All of us make promises to others and to ourselves almost every day. Before leaving for work in the morning, a husband might tell his wife, "I'll pick up the dry cleaning on my way home." A mother with several small children might promise to take them out for a walk in the afternoon after a quiet morning at home.

If you think about it for a moment, we all make promises to ourselves many times a day. "I'm going to finish that project at work today", we might say as we arrive at the office. Or, "I'm finally going to get around to cleaning out the refrigerator", we might tell ourselves after several weeks of procrastination.

Making promises is clearly an important part of our daily life. We commit ourselves to do something, and we sincerely intend to carry it through. We also expect others – particularly those we respect and love – to fulfil their promises.

Besides these daily promises to ourselves and others, we also make serious commitments that involve long-term or even lifelong promises. Usually we make these kinds of promises only after carefully thinking through the implications and consequences of our decision. For instance, a young couple might wait several months or years before they exchange solemn vows at the altar. These vows are binding throughout the life of both partners and should not be approached casually.

The hard reality of human promises, though, is that we can't absolutely rely on them. Even with the best of intentions, we may fail to fulfil them because of circumstances beyond our control. A highly rated long distance runner might train for the Olympics only to have her dreams shattered when she slips and sprains her ankle in the trial heats. Or a reliable and loving father of a growing family may be stricken with multiple sclerosis. Within a matter of months, he finds himself unable to work and provide for his family.

But even if we fail or others fail us – even if unforeseen circumstances bring misfortune our way – we still have good reason to hope as Christians. That hope is sure because it is founded on God's faithful promises which have been recorded in the Scriptures.

Put simply, God is *always* faithful. Unlike us, he has limitless power, and authority, and he backs up every promise he makes with his integrity. Whatever God has promised, we can be certain that he will fulfil it at the appropriate time.

The marvellous and amazing truth is that God has given us literally hundreds of promises in his Word, the holy Scriptures. There we find personal promises from God to each of us as his sons and daughters. We also find many promises God has made to the whole people of God, the Church.

These God-given promises cover literally every area of our life – our physical well-being, our material needs, and our emotional, social, psychological and spiritual life. God even promises us unheard-of-favours and blessings if we remain faithful to him.

Consider some of the many life-giving promises that God makes to us in the Bible. He promises us his loving and abiding presence, even in hard times. He promises us his fatherly care and protection every moment of our life. He offers those who sincerely seek him the immeasurable gift of salvation and eternal life. In fact, he promises us as Christians that we will literally reign with Christ in heaven for ever as kings and priests! He promises us courage and strength when we feel weak and helpless. As members of his Church, he promises us close and supportive personal relationships with our brothers and sisters in Christ.

Scripture tells us that God in his good pleasure seeks to give us all these good things and much more. His promises are truly exceeding in greatness. As the apostle Peter tells us:

> His divine power has bestowed on us everything that makes for life and devotion, through the knowledge of him who called us by his own glory and power. Through these, he has bestowed on us the precious and very great promises, so that through them you may come to share in the divine nature, after escaping from the corruption that is in the world because of evil desire. (2 Peter 1:3–4)

The good news is that God's exceedingly great promises to us will be fulfilled in his time, even if we presently seem to be facing insurmountable obstacles. In his own day, the prophet Ezekiel told the disheartened Jewish people who were in exile:

Thus says the Lord God: O my people, I will open your graves and have you rise from them, and bring you back to the land of Israel. Then you shall know that I am the Lord, when I open your graves and have you rise from them, O my people! I will put my spirit in you that you may live, and I will settle you in the land; thus you shall know that I am the Lord. *I have promised, and I will do it*, says the Lord. (Ezekiel 37:12–14, emphasis added)

That Word in Scripture remains true for us today. It shows us that God wants to impart his very life to us. We have his word on it.

Scripture is not just meant for devotional reading and meditation. Rather, the words of sacred Scripture are meant to become the very source of our strength and our hope:

Such is the force and power of the Word of God that it can serve the Church as her support and vigour, and the children of the Church as strength for their faith, food for the soul, and a pure and lasting fount of spiritual life. Scripture verifies in a most perfect way the words: "The Word of God is living and active" (Heb 4:12), and "is able to build you up and to give you the inheritance among all those who are sanctified" (Acts 20:32).

How can this book help you receive the life-giving Word of God? If you use it as part of your regular prayer life, this book of Bible promises can help you understand and claim God's promises for yourself, your family, and your friends.

First you need to get a sense of how the book is organized. The promises are arranged by category with four or five subheadings under each one. For instance, *God's Love, God's Abiding Presence, God's Mercy and Compassion* and *God's Faithfulness* are the four subheadings under the category *God's Attitude towards Us*. The categories run the gamut from God's promise of salvation and our own personal needs and relationships, to God's promises to the Church.

Scripture Promises is ideal for personal use. You can either use it as a handy reference work to turn to in a moment of need, or you can read through the promises under a certain category for daily scriptural prayer and meditation. For example, suppose a young woman doubts God's love for her. She can make a practice of turning to the subheading on God's love and other related subheadings whenever she begins to doubt his love. Or she could decide to spend time every day meditating on some of the promises listed under the subheading on God's love.

This Bible promise book is also ideal for family use. You can use it during times of family devotion to help strengthen and encourage family members in a certain area. Parents could spend some time teaching their children about the promises God has made to his people, for example, by turning to the category titled God's Promises to the Church. Or maybe you have a family member or a close friend who is facing a personal problem. Sharing about God's promises in the area of difficulty may be just the encouragement he or she needs to trust in God's care and provision.

However you incorporate it into your regular prayer life, *Scripture Promises* will remain an invaluable help to you, your family and your friends in claiming and treasuring God's promises for many years to come.

Carmen Rojas
Compiler

I

God's Attitude towards Us

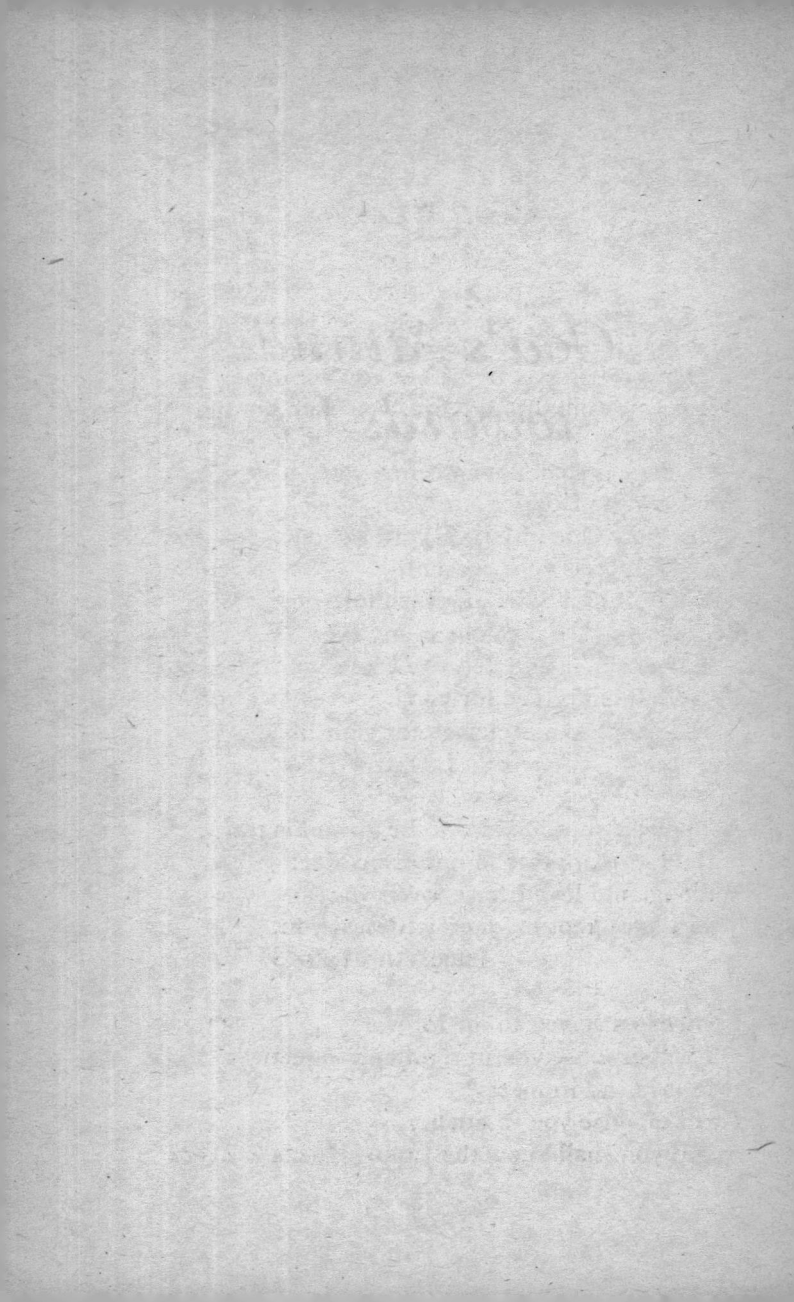

1

God's Love

Fear not, for I have redeemed you;
  I have called you by name: you are mine.
When you walk through fire, you shall not be
    burned;
  the flames shall not consume you.
For I am the LORD, your God,
  the Holy One of Israel, your saviour.
I give Egypt as your ransom,
  Ethiopia and Seba in return for you.
Because you are precious in my eyes
  and glorious, and because I love you.
I give men in return for you
  and peoples in exchange for your life.
             ISAIAH 43:1b–4

As Israel comes forward to be given his rest,
  the LORD appears to him from afar:
With age-old love I have loved you;
  so I have kept my mercy toward you.
             JEREMIAH 31:2b–3

I will espouse you to me forever:
  I will espouse you in right and in justice,
  in love and in mercy;
I will espouse you in fidelity,
  and you shall know the LORD. HOSEA 2:21–22

I will heal their defection,
  I will love them freely;
  for my wrath is turned away from them.
I will be like the dew for Israel:
  He shall blossom like the lily;
He shall strike root like the Lebanon cedar,
  and put forth his shoots. HOSEA 14:5–7a

For God so loved the world that he gave his only Son, so that everyone who believes in him might not perish but might have eternal life. For God did not send his Son into the world to condemn the world, but that the world might be saved through him. Whoever believes in him will not be condemned, but whoever does not believe has already been condemned, because he has not believed in the name of the only Son of God. JOHN 3:16–18

"I give you a new commandment: love one another. As I have loved you, so you also should love one another. This is how all will know that you are my disciples, if you have love for one another."

JOHN 13:34–35

Therefore, since we have been justified by faith, we have peace with God through our Lord Jesus Christ, through whom we have gained access [by faith] to this grace in which we stand, and we boast in hope of the glory of God. Not only that, but we even boast of our afflictions, knowing that affliction produces endurance, and endurance, proven character, and proven character, hope, and hope does not disappoint, because the love of God has been poured out into our hearts through the holy spirit that has been given to us. ROMANS 5:1–5

For Christ, while we were still helpless, yet died at the appointed time for the ungodly. Indeed, only with difficulty does one die for a just person, though perhaps for a good person one might even find courage to die. But God proves his love for us in that while we were still sinners Christ died for us. ROMANS 5:6–8

What then shall we say to this? If God is for us, who can be against us? He who did not spare his own Son but handed him over for us all, how will he not also give us everything else along with him? Who will bring a charge against God's chosen ones? It is God who acquits us. Who will condemn? It is Christ [Jesus] who died, rather, was raised, who also is at the right hand of God, who indeed intercedes for us. What will separate us from the love of Christ? Will anguish, or distress, or persecution, or famine, or nakedness, or peril, or the sword? As it is written:
  "For your sake we are being slain all the day;
  We are looked upon as sheep to be slaughtered."
No, in all these things we conquer overwhelmingly through him who loved us. For I am convinced that neither death, nor life, nor angels, not principalities, nor present things, nor future things, nor powers, nor height, nor depth, nor any other creature will be able to separate us from the love of God in Christ Jesus our Lord. ROMANS 8:31–39

See what love the Father has bestowed on us that we may be called the children of God. Yet so we are.

The reason the world does not know us is that it did not know him. Beloved, we are God's children now; what we shall be has not yet been revealed. We do know that when it is revealed we shall be like him for we shall see him as he is. Everyone who has this hope based on him makes himself pure, as he is pure.

1 JOHN 3:1–3

Beloved, let us love one another, because love is of God; everyone who loves is begotten by God and knows God. Whoever is without love does not know God, for God is love. In this way the love of God was revealed to us: God sent his only Son into the world so that we might have life through him. In this is love: not that we have loved God, but that he loved us and sent his Son as expiation for our sins. Beloved, if God so loved us, we also must love one another.

1 JOHN 4:7–11

This is how you can know the Spirit of God: every spirit that acknowledges Jesus Christ come in the flesh belongs to God, and every spirit that does not acknowledge Jesus does not belong to God. This is the spirit of the antichrist that, as you heard, is to come, but in fact is already in the world. You belong to God, children, and you have conquered them, for the one who is in you is greater than the one who is in the world. They belong to the world; accordingly, their teaching belongs to the world, and the world listens to them. We belong to God, and anyone who knows God listens to us, while anyone who does not belong to God refuses to hear us. This is how we

know the spirit of truth and the spirit of deceit.
1 JOHN 4:2–6

We have come to know and to believe in the love God
has for us.

God is love, and whoever remains in love remains
in God and God in him. In this is love brought to
perfection among us, that we have confidence on the
day of judgement because as he is, so are we in this
world. There is no fear in love, but perfect love drives
out fear because fear has to do with punishment, and
so one who fears is not yet perfect in love. We love
because he first loved us. 1 JOHN 4:16–19

Indeed, before you the whole universe
    is as a grain from a balance,
    or a drop of morning dew come down upon the
        earth.
But you have mercy on all, because you can do all
        things;
    and you overlook the sins of men that they may
        repent.
For you love all things that are
    and loathe nothing that you have made;
    for what you hated, you would not have fashioned.
And how could a thing remain, unless you willed it;
    or be preserved, had it not been called forth by
        you?
But you spare all things, because they
    are yours, O LORD and lover of souls,
    for your imperishable spirit is in all things!
                    WISDOM 11:22–26; 12:1

For this reason I kneel before the Father, from whom every family in heaven and on earth is named, that he may grant you in accord with the riches of his glory to be strengthened with power through his Spirit in the inner self, and that Christ may dwell in your hearts through faith; that you, rooted and grounded in love, may have strength to comprehend with all the holy ones what is the breadth and length and height and depth, and to know the love of Christ that surpasses knowledge, so that you may be filled with all the fullness of God. EPHESIANS 3:14–19

For he who has become your husband is your Maker;
  his name is the LORD of hosts;
Your redeemer is the Holy One of Israel,
  called God of all the earth.
The LORD calls you back,
  like a wife forsaken and grieved in spirit,
A wife married in youth and then cast off,
  says your God.
For a brief moment I abandoned you,
  but with great tenderness I will take you back.
In an outburst of wrath, for a moment
  I hid my face from you;
But with enduring love I take pity on you,
  says the LORD, your redeemer. ISAIAH 54:5–8

2

God's Abiding Presence

Can a mother forget her infant,
    be without tenderness for the child of her womb?
Even should she forget,
    I will never forget you.
See, upon the palms of my hands I have written your
       name;
    your walls are ever before me. ISAIAH 49:15–16

And the Word became flesh
    and made his dwelling among us,
    and we saw his glory,
    the glory as of the Father's only Son,
    full of grace and truth. JOHN 1:14

"Remain in me, as I remain in you. Just as a branch
cannot bear fruit on its own unless it remains on the
vine, so neither can you unless you remain in me. I
am the vine, you are the branches. Whoever remains
in me and I in him will bear much fruit, because
without me you can do nothing." JOHN 15:4–5

"If you remain in me and my words remain in you,
ask for whatever you want and it will be done for you.
By this is my Father glorified, that you bear much
fruit and become my disciples. As the Father loves
me, so I also love you. Remain in my love. If you

keep my commandments, you will remain in my love, just as I have kept my Father's commandments and remain in his love." JOHN 15:7–10

None of us lives for oneself, and no one dies for oneself. For if we live, we live for the Lord, and if we die, we die for the Lord; so then, whether we live or die, we are the Lord's. For this is why Christ died and came to life, that he might be Lord of both the dead and the living. ROMANS 14:7–9

"The God who made the world and all that is in it, the Lord of heaven and earth, does not dwell in sanctuaries made by human hands, nor is he served by human hands because he needs anything. Rather it is he who gives to everyone life and breath and everything. He made from one the whole human race to dwell on the entire surface of the earth, and he fixed the ordered seasons and the boundaries of their regions, so that people might seek God, even perhaps grope for him and find him, though indeed he is not far from any one of us. For 'In him we live and move and have our being,' as even some of your poets have said, 'For we too are his offspring.'" ACTS 17:24–28

This is how we know that we remain in him, and he in us, that he has given us of his Spirit. Moreover, we have seen and testify that the Father sent his Son as saviour of the world. Whoever acknowledges that Jesus is the Son of God, God remains in him and he in God. We have come to know and to believe in the love God has for us.

God is love, and whoever remains in love remains in God and God in him. 1 JOHN 4:13–16

The four living creatures, each of them with six wings, were covered with eyes inside and out. Day and night they do not stop exclaiming:
   "'Holy, holy, holy is the Lord God almighty,
   Who was, and who is, and who is to come."
                                         REVELATION 4:8

I decree that throughout my royal domain the God of Daniel is to be reverenced and feared:
"For he is the living God, enduring forever;
   his kingdom shall not be destroyed,
   and his dominion shall be without end.
He is a deliverer and saviour,
   working signs and wonders in heaven and on earth,
   and he delivered Daniel from the lions' power."
                                         DANIEL 6:27–28

"And behold, I am with you always, until the end of the age." MATTHEW 28:20b

. . ."Amen, amen, I say to you, unless you eat the flesh of the Son of Man and drink his blood, you do not have life within you. Whoever eats my flesh and drinks my blood has eternal life, and I will raise him on the last day. For my flesh is true food, and my blood is true drink. Whoever eats my flesh and drinks my blood remains in me and I in him. Just as the living Father sent me and I have life because of the Father, so also the one who feeds on me will have life because of me." JOHN 6:53–57

Though the proud scoff bitterly at me,
    I turn not away from your law. PSALM 119:51

Where can I go from your spirit?
    from your presence where can I flee?
If I go up to the heavens, you are there;
    if I sink to the nether world, you are present there.
If I take the wings of the dawn,
    if I settle at the farthest limits of the sea,
Even there your hand shall guide me,
    and your right hand hold me fast.
If I say, "Surely the darkness shall hide me,
    and night shall be my light" –
For you darkness itself is not dark,
    and night shines as the day.
[Darkness and light are the same.] PSALM 139:7–12

For a child is born to us, a son is given us;
    upon his shoulder dominion rests.
They name him Wonder-Counsellor, God-Hero,
    Father-Forever, Prince of Peace.
His dominion is vast
    and forever peaceful,
From David's throne, and over his kingdom,
    which he confirms and sustains
By judgement and justice,
    both now and forever.
The zeal of the LORD of hosts will do this!
                                    ISAIAH 9:5–6

Indeed he neither slumbers nor sleeps,
    the guardian of Israel.
The LORD is your guardian; the LORD is your shade;

He is beside you at your right hand.
The sun shall not harm you by day,
  nor the moon by night.
The LORD will guard you from all evil;
  he will guard your life.
The LORD will guard your coming and your going,
  both now and forever. PSALM 121:4–8

The LORD is the eternal God,
  creator of the ends of the earth.
He does not faint nor grow weary,
  and his knowledge is beyond scrutiny.
                    ISAIAH 40:28b

Indeed the LORD will be there with us, majestic;
  yes, the LORD our judge, the LORD our lawgiver,
  the LORD our king, he it is who will save us.
                    ISAIAH 33:22

. . ."Do not be afraid. I am the first and the last, the one who lives. Once I was dead, but now I am alive forever and ever. I hold the keys to death and the netherworld." REVELATION 1:17b–18

3

God's Mercy and Compassion

For the Lord's rejection
  does not last forever;
Though he punishes, he takes pity,
  in the abundance of his mercies;
He has no joy in afflicting
  or grieving the sons of men.
          LAMENTATIONS 3:31–33

Thus says the Lord God to Jerusalem: By origin and
birth you are of the land of Canaan; your father was
an Amorite and your mother a Hittite. As for your
birth, the day you were born your navel cord was not
cut; you were neither washed with water nor anointed,
nor were you rubbed with salt, nor swathed in swad-
dling clothes. No one looked on you with pity or
compassion to do any of these things for you. Rather,
you were thrown out on the ground as something
loathsome, the day you were born.

Then I passed by and saw you weltering in your
blood. I said to you: Live in your blood and grow like
a plant in the field. You grew and developed, you
came to the age of puberty; your breasts were formed,
your hair had grown, but you were still stark naked.
Again I passed by you and saw that you were now old
enough for love. So I spread the corner of my cloak
over you to cover your nakedness; I swore an oath to

you and entered into a covenant with you; you became mine, says the Lord God. EZEKIEL 16:3–8

My heart is overwhelmed,
   my pity is stirred.
I will not give vent to my blazing anger.
   I will not destroy Ephraim again;
For I am God and not man,
   the Holy One present among you;
   I will not let the flames consume you.
HOSEA 11:8b–9

Who is there like you, the God who removes guilt
   and pardons sin for the remnant of his inheritance;
Who does not persist in anger forever,
   but delights rather in clemency,
And will again have compassion on us,
   treading underfoot our guilt?
You will cast into the depths of the sea
   all our sins;
You will show faithfulness to Jacob,
   and grace to Abraham,
As you have sworn to our fathers
   from days of old. MICAH 7:18–20

So it depends not upon a person's will or exertion, but upon God, who shows mercy. For the scripture says to Pharaoh, "This is why I have raised you up, to show my power through you that my name may be proclaimed throughout the earth." Consequently, he has mercy upon whom he wills, and he hardens whom he wills. ROMANS 9:16–18

You will say to me then, "Why [then] does he still find fault? For who can oppose his will?" But who indeed are you, a human being, to talk back to God? Will what is made say to its maker, "Why have you created me so?" Or does not the potter have a right over the clay, to make out of the same lump one vessel for a noble purpose and another for an ignoble one? What if God, wishing to show his wrath and make known his power, has endured with much patience the vessels of wrath made for destruction? This was to make known the riches of his glory to the vessels of mercy, which he has prepared previously for glory, namely, us whom he has called, not only from the Jews but also from the Gentiles. ROMANS 9:19–24

But as you are just, you govern all things justly;
   you regard it as unworthy of your power
   to punish one who has incurred no blame.
For your might is the source of justice;
   your mastery over all things makes you lenient to
      all.
For you show your might when the
   perfection of your power is disbelieved;
   and in those who know you, you rebuke temerity.
But though you are master of might, you judge with
      clemency,
   and with much lenience you govern us;
   for power, whenever you will, attends you.
                    WISDOM 12:15–18

Alleluia.
Give thanks to the LORD, for he is good,
   for his mercy endures forever;

Give thanks to the God of gods,
    for his mercy endures forever;
Give thanks to the Lord of lords,
    for his mercy endures forever;
Who alone does great wonders,
    for his mercy endures forever;
Who made the heavens in wisdom,
    for his mercy endures forever;
Who spread out the earth upon the waters,
    for his mercy endures forever;
Who made the great lights,
    for his mercy endures forever;
The sun to rule over the day,
    for his mercy endures forever;
The moon and the stars to rule over the night,
    for his mercy endures forever. PSALM 136:1–9

Who remembered us in our abjection,
    for his mercy endures forever;
And freed us from our foes,
    for his mercy endures forever;
Who gives food to all flesh,
    for his mercy endures forever;
Give thanks to the God of heaven,
    for his mercy endures forever. PSALM 136:23–26

When you turn back to him with all your heart,
    to do what is right before him,
Then he will turn back to you,
    and no longer hide his face from you.
So not consider what he has done for you,
    and praise him with full voice. TOBIT 13:6a

It is I, I, who wipe out,
    for my own sake, your offences;
    your sins I remember no more. ISAIAH 43:25

Remember this, O Jacob,
    you, O Israel, who are my servant!
I formed you to be a servant to me;
    O Israel, by me you shall never be forgotten:
I have brushed away your offences like a cloud,
    your sins like a mist;
    return to me, for I have redeemed you.
                ISAIAH 44:21–22

He said: They are indeed my people,
    children who are not disloyal;
So he became their saviour
    in their every affliction.
It was not a messenger or an angel,
    but he himself who saved them.
Because of his love and pity
    he redeemed them himself,
Lifting them and carrying them
    all the days of old. ISAIAH 63:8–9

"What man among you have a hundred sheep and losing one of them would not leave the ninety-nine in the desert and go after the lost one until he finds it? And when he does find it, he sets it on his shoulders with great joy and, upon his arrival home, he calls together his friends and neighbours and says to them, 'Rejoice with me because I have found my lost sheep.' I tell you, in just the same way there will be more joy in heaven over one sinner who repents than over ninety-nine righteous people who have no need for repentance." LUKE 15:4–7

"Or what woman having ten coins and losing one would not light a lamp and sweep the house, searching carefully until she finds it? And when she does find it, she calls together her friends and neighbors and says to them, 'Rejoice with me because I have found the coin that I lost.' In just the same way, I tell you, there will be rejoicing among the angels of God over one sinner who repents." LUKE 15:8–10

. . .Zacchaeus stood there and said to the Lord, "Behold, half of my possessions, Lord, I shall give to the poor, and if I have extorted anything from anyone I shall repay it four times over." And Jesus said to him, "Today salvation has come to this house because this man too is a descendant of Abraham. For the Son of Man has come to seek and to save what was lost."

LUKE 19:8–10

4

God's Faithfulness

The favours of the LORD are not exhausted,
    his mercies are not spent;
They are renewed each morning,
    so great is his faithfulness.
                    LAMENTATIONS 3:22–23

"Though the grass withers and the flower wilts,
    the word of our God stands forever." ISAIAH 40:8

O LORD, your kindness reaches to heaven;
    Your faithfulness, to the clouds.
Your justice is like the mountains of God;
    Your judgments, like the mighty deep;
    man and beast you save, O LORD.
How precious is your kindness, O God!
    The children of men take refuge in the shadow of
        your wings,
They have their fill of the prime gifts of your house;
    from your delightful stream you give them to
        drink.
For with you is the fountain of life,
    and in your light we see light. PSALM 36:6–10

"Blessed be the LORD who has given rest to his
people Israel, just as he promised. Not a single word
has gone unfilfilled of the entire generous promise he

made through his servant Moses. May the LORD, our God, be with us as he was with our fathers and may he not forsake us nor cast us off. May he draw our hearts to himself, that we may follow him in everything and keep the commands, statutes, and ordinances which he enjoined on our fathers. May this prayer I have offered to the LORD, our God, be present to him day and night, that he may uphold the cause of his servant and of his people Israel as each day requires, that all the peoples of the earth may know the LORD is God and there is no other."

1 KINGS 8:56–60

This saying is trustworthy:
If we have died with him
  we shall also live with him;
if we persevere
  we shall also reign with him.
But if we deny him
  he will deny us.
If we are unfaithful
  he remains faithful,
    for he cannot deny himself. 2 TIMOTHY 2:11–13

The one who calls you is faithful, and he will also accomplish it. 1 THESSALONIANS 5:24

It was because the LORD loved you and because of his fidelity to the oath he had sworn to your fathers, that he brought you out with his strong hand from the place of slavery, and ransomed you from the hand of Pharaoh, king of Egypt. Understand, then, that the LORD, your God, is God indeed, the faithful God

who keeps his merciful covenant down to the thou-
sandth generation toward those who love him and
keep his commandments, . . . DEUTERONOMY 7:8–9

Though the mountains leave their place
    and the hills be shaken,
My love shall never leave you
    nor my covenant of peace be shaken,
    says the LORD, who has mercy on you.
                                         ISAIAH 54:10

God is faithful, and by him you were called to
fellowship with his Son, Jesus Christ our Lord.
                                         1 CORINTHIANS 1:9

The Lord does not delay his promise, as some regard
"delay", but he is patient with you, not wishing that
any should perish but that all should come to repentance. 2 PETER 3:9

"Blessed be the Lord, the God of Israel,
    for he has visited and brought redemption to his
        people.
He has raised up a horn for our salvation
    within the house of David his servant,
even as he promised through the mouth of his holy
        prophets from of old;
    salvation from our enemies and from the hand of
        all who hate us,
to show mercy to our fathers
    and to be mindful of his holy covenant
and of the oath he swore to Abraham our father,

and to grant us that, rescued from the hand of
    enemies,
without fear we might worship him in holiness and
    righteousness
    before him all our days.
And you, child, will be called prophet of the Most
    High,
    for you will go before the Lord to prepare his
    ways,
to give his people knowledge of salvation
    through the forgiveness of their sins,
because of the tender mercy of our God
    by which the daybreak from on high will visit us
to shine on those who sit in darkness and death's
    shadow,
    to guide our feet into the path of peace."
LUKE 1:68–79

If we acknowledge our sins, he is faithful and just and
will forgive our sins and cleanse us from every wrongdoing. 1 JOHN 1:9

Let us hold unwaveringly to our confession that gives
us hope, for he who made the promise is trustworthy.
HEBREWS 10:23

But the Lord is faithful; he will strengthen you and
guard you from the evil one. 2 THESSALONIANS 3:3

I will give thanks to you among the peoples, O Lord,
    I will chant your praise among the nations,
For your kindness towers to the heavens,
    and your faithfulness to the skies. PSALM 57:10–11

Every word of God is tested;
  he is a shield to those who take refuge in him.
                                    PROVERBS 30:5

For he spoke, and it was made;
  he commanded, and it stood forth . . .
But the plan of the LORD stands forever;
  the design of his heart, through all generations.
                                    PSALM 33:9, 11

Your promise is very sure,
  and your servant loves it . . .
Permanence is your word's chief trait;
  each of your just ordinances is everlasting.
                                    PSALM 119:140, 160

The promises of the LORD are sure,
  like tried silver, freed from dross, sevenfold
    refined. PSALM 12:7

God is not man that he should speak falsely,
  nor human, that he should change his mind.
Is he one to speak and not act,
  to decree and not fulfil? NUMBERS 23:19

For just as from the heavens
  the rain and snow come down
And do not return there
  till they have watered the earth,
  making it fertile and fruitful,
Giving seed to him who sows
  and bread to him who eats,
So shall my word be

that goes forth from my mouth;
It shall not return to me void,
    but shall do my will,
    achieving the end for which I sent it.
                        ISAIAH 55:10–11

"Amen, I say to you, this generation will not pass away until all these things have taken place. Heaven and earth will pass away, but my words will not pass away." MATTHEW 24:34–35

For the gifts and the call of God are irrevocable.
                        ROMANS 11:29

II

God's Promise
of Salvation

5

Eternal Life

But now that you have been freed from sin and have become slaves of God, the benefit that you have leads to sanctification, and its end is eternal life. For the wages of sin is death, but the gift of God is eternal life in Christ Jesus our Lord. ROMANS 6:22–23

"And this is the promise that he made us: eternal life. I write you these things about those who would deceive you. As for you, the anointing that you received from him remains in you, so that you do not need anyone to teach you. But his anointing teaches you about everything and is true and not false; just as it taught you, remain in him. 1 JOHN 2:25–27

And this is the testimony: God gave us eternal life, and this life is in his Son. Whoever possesses the Son has life; whoever does not possess the Son of God does not have life. 1 JOHN 5:11–12

We know that we belong to God, and the whole world is under the power of the evil one. We also know that the Son of God has come and has given us discernment to know the one who is true. And we are in the one who is true, in his Son Jesus Christ. He is the true God and eternal life. 1 JOHN 5:19–20

"And this is the will of the one who sent me, that I should not lose anything of what he gave me, but that I should raise it [on] the last day. For this is the will of my Father, that everyone who sees the Son and believes in him may have eternal life, and I shall raise him [on] the last day." JOHN 6:39–40

Now someone approached him and said, "Teacher, what good must I do to gain eternal life?" He answered him, "Why do you ask me about the good? There is only One who is good. If you wish to enter into life, keep the commandments." He asked him, "Which ones?" And Jesus replied, '"You shall not kill; you shall not commit adultery; you shall not steal; you shall not bear false witness; honour your father and your mother'; and 'you shall love your neighbour as yourself.'" The young man said to him, "All of these I have observed. What do I still lack?" Jesus said to him, "If you wish to be perfect, go, sell what you have and give to [the] poor, and you will have treasure in heaven. Then come, follow me." MATTHEW 19:16–21

For God so loved the world that he gave his only Son, so that everyone who believes in him might not perish but might have eternal life. JOHN 3:16

"Amen, amen, I say to you, whoever believes has eternal life." JOHN 6:47

"Amen, amen, I say to you, whoever hears my word and believes in the one who sent me has eternal life and will not come to condemnation, but has passed from death to life." JOHN 5:24

"My sheep hear my voice; I know them, and they follow me. I give them eternal life, and they shall never perish. No one can take them out of my hand."

JOHN 10:27–28

Jesus said to them, "Amen, amen, I say to you, unless you eat the flesh of the Son of Man and drink his blood, you do not have life within you. Whoever eats my flesh and drinks my blood has eternal life, and I will raise him on the last day. For my flesh is true food, and my blood is true drink. Whoever eats my flesh and drinks my blood remains in me and I in him. Just as the living Father sent me and I have life because of the Father, so also the one who feeds on me will have life because of me." JOHN 6:53–57

Paul, a slave of God and apostle of Jesus Christ for the sake of the faith of God's chosen ones and the recognition of religious truth, in the hope of eternal life that God, who does not lie, promised before time began, who indeed at the proper time revealed his word in the proclamation with which I was entrusted by the command of God our saviour, to Titus, my true child in our common faith: grace and peace from God the Father and Christ Jesus our saviour.

TITUS 1:1–4

If the Spirit of the one who raised Jesus from the dead dwells in you, the one who raised Christ from the dead will give life to your mortal bodies also, through his Spirit that dwells in you. ROMANS 8:11

There was a scholar of the law who stood up to test him and said, "Teacher, what must I do to inherit eternal life?" Jesus said to him, "What is written in the law? How do you read it?" He said in reply, "You shall love the Lord, your God, with all your heart, with all your being, with all your strength, and with all your mind, and your neighbour as yourself." He replied to him, "You have answered correctly; do this and you will live." LUKE 10:25–28

The Father loves the Son and has given everything over to him. Whoever believes in the Son has eternal life, but whoever disobeys the Son will not see life, but the wrath of God remains upon him.

JOHN 3:35–36

By your stubbornness and impenitent heart, you are storing up wrath for yourself for the day of wrath and revelation of the just judgement of God, who will repay everyone according to his works: eternal life to those who seek glory, honour, and immortality through perseverance in good works, but wrath and fury to those who selfishly disobey the truth and obey wickedness. Yes, affliction and distress will come upon every human being who does evil, Jew first and then Greek. But there will be glory, honour, and peace for everyone who does good, Jew first and then Greek. There is no partiality with God. ROMANS 2:5–11

For just as through the disobedience of one person the many were made sinners, so through the obedience of one the many will be made righteous. The law entered in so that transgression might increase but, where sin increased, grace overflowed all the more, so that, as sin reigned in death, grace also might reign through justification for eternal life through Jesus Christ our Lord. ROMANS 5:19–21

But you, man of God, avoid all this. Instead, pursue righteousness, devotion, faith, love, patience, and gentleness. Compete well for the faith. Lay hold of eternal life, to which you were called when you made the noble confession in the presence of many witnesses. TIMOTHY 6:11–12

But when the kindness and generous love
   of God our saviour appeared,
not because of any righteous deeds we had done
   but because of his mercy,
he saved us through the bath of rebirth
   and renewal by the holy Spirit,
whom he richly poured out on us
   through Jesus Christ our saviour,
so that we might be justified by his grace
   and become heirs in hope of eternal life.
This saying is truthworthy. TITUS 3:4–8

We know that we have passed from death to life because we love our brothers. Whoever does not love remains in death. Everyone who hates his brother is a murderer, and you know that no murderer has eternal life remaining in him. JOHN 3:14–15

I write these things to you so that you may know that you have eternal life, you who believe in the name of the Son of God. And we have this confidence in him, that if we ask anything according to his will, he hears us. JOHN 5:13–14

But you, beloved, build yourselves up in your most holy faith; pray in the holy Spirit. Keep yourselves in the love of God and wait for the mercy of our Lord Jesus Christ that leads to eternal life. JUDE 20–21

Jesus told her, "I am the resurrection and the life; whoever believes in me, even if he dies, will live, and everyone who lives and believes in me will never die. Do you believe this?" She said to him, "Yes, Lord. I have come to believe that you are the Messiah, the Son of God, the one who is coming into the world."

JOHN 11:25–27

6

Forgiveness and Reconciliation

Indeed, if, while we were enemies, we were reconciled to God through the death of his Son, how much more, once reconciled, will we be saved by his life. Not only that, but we also boast of God through our Lord Jesus Christ, through whom we have now received reconciliation. ROMANS 5:10–11

If we acknowledge our sins, he is faithful and just and will forgive our sins and cleanse us from every wrongdoing. If we say, "We have not sinned," we make him a liar, and his word is not in us. 1 JOHN 1:9–10

He delivered us from the power of darkness and transferred us to the kingdom of his beloved Son, in whom we have redemption, the forgiveness of sins.
COLOSSIANS 1:13–14

For him in all the fullness was pleased to dwell,
    and through him to reconcile all things for him,
    making peace by the blood of his cross
    [through him], whether those on earth or those in
    heaven.
And who you once were alienated and hostile in mind because of evil deeds he has now reconciled in his fleshly body through his death, to present you holy, without blemish, and irreproachable before him,

provided that you persevere in the faith, firmly grounded, stable, and not shifting from the hope of the gospel that you heard, which has been preached to every creature under heaven, of which I, Paul, am a minister. COLOSSIANS 1:19–23

My children, I am writing this to you so that you may not commit sin. But if anyone does sin, we have an Advocate with the Father, Jesus Christ the righteous one. 1 JOHN 2:1

You were buried with him in baptism, in which you were also raised from him through faith in the power of God, who raised him from the dead. And even when you were dead [in] trangressions and the uncircumcision of your flesh, he brought you to life along with him, having forgiven us all our transgressions; obliterating the bond against us, with its legal claims, which was opposed to us, he also removed it from our midst, nailing it to the cross; despoiling the principalities and the powers, he made a public spectacle of them, leading them away in triumph by it.

COLOSSIANS 2:12–15

. . . who gave himself for us to deliver us from all lawlessness and to cleanse for himself a people as his own, eager to do what is good. TITUS 2:14

"To him all the prophets bear witness, that everyone who believes in him will receive forgiveness of sins through his name." ACTS 10:43

But the one whom God raised up did not see corruption. You must know, my brothers, that through him forgiveness of sins is being proclaimed to you, [and] in regard to everything from which you could not be justified under the law of Moses, in him every believer is justified. ACTS 13:37–39

Happy is he whose fault is taken away,
   whose sin is covered.
Happy the man to whom the LORD imputes not guilt,
   in whose spirit there is no guile.
As long as I would not speak, my bones wasted away
   with groaning all the day,
For day and night your hand was heavy upon me;
   my strength was dried up as by the heat of
     summer.
Then I acknowledged my sin to you,
   my guilt I covered not.
I said, "I confess my faults to the LORD,"
   and you took away the guilt of my sin.
                      PSALM 32:1–5

Come now, let us set things right,
   says the LORD:
Though your sins be like scarlet,
   they may become white as snow;
Though they be crimson red,
   they may become white as wool.
If you are willing, and obey,
   you shall eat the good things of the land;
But if you refuse and resist,

the sword shall consume you:
for the mouth of the LORD has spoken!
ISAIAH 1:18–20

He pardons all your iniquities,
    he heals all your ills,
He redeems your life from destruction,
    he crowns you with kindness and compassion, . . .
Merciful and gracious is the LORD,
    slow to anger and abounding in kindness.
He will not always chide,
    nor does he keep his wrath forever.
Not according to our sins does he deal with us,
    nor does he requite us according to our crimes.
For as the heavens are high above the earth,
    so surpassing is his kindness toward those who fear
        him.
As far as the east is from the west,
    so far has he put our transgressions from us.
PSALM 103:3–4, 8–12

So whoever is in Christ is a new creation: the old things have passed away; behold, new things have come. And all this is from God, who has reconciled us to himself through Christ and given us the ministry of reconciliation, namely, God was reconciling the world to himself in Christ, not counting their trespasses against them and entrusting to us the message of reconciliation . . . For our sake he made him to be sin who did not know sin, so that we might become the righteousness of God in him.

CORINTHIANS 5:17–19, 21

In him we have redemption by his blood, the forgiveness of transgressions, in accord with the riches of his grace . . . EPHESIANS 1:7

You were dead in your transgressions and sins in which you once lived following the age of this world, following the ruler of the power of the air, the spirit that is now at work in the disobedient. All of us once lived among them in the desires of our flesh, following the wishes of the flesh and the impulses, and we were by nature children of wrath, like the rest. But God, who is rich in mercy, because of the great love he had for us, even when we were dead in our transgressions, brought us to life with Christ (by grace you have been saved), raised us up with him, and seated us with him in the heavens in Christ Jesus, that in the ages to come he might show the immeasurable riches of his grace in his kindness to us in Christ Jesus.

EPHESIANS 2:1–7

Therefore, remember that at one time you, Gentiles in the flesh, called the uncircumcision by those called the circumcision, which is done in the flesh by human hands, were at that time without Christ, alienated from the community of Israel and strangers to the covenants of promise, without hope and without God in the world. But now is Christ Jesus you who once were far off have become near by the blood of Christ.

EPHESIANS 2:11–13

For he is our peace, he who made both one and broke down the dividing wall of enmity, through his flesh, abolishing the law with its commandments and legal claims, that he might create in himself one new person in place of the two, thus establishing peace, and might reconcile both with God, in one body, through the cross, putting that enmity to death by it. He came and preached peace to you who were far off and peace to those who were near, for through him we both have access in one Spirit to the Father.

EPHESIANS 2:14–18

God exalted him at his right hand as leader and saviour to grant Israel repentance and forgiveness of sins.

ACTS 5:31

7

Salvation through Jesus Christ

For Christ, while we were still helpless, yet died at the appointed time for the ungodly. Indeed, only with difficulty does one die for a just person, though perhaps for a good person one might even find courage to die. But God proves his love for us in that while we were still sinners Christ died for us. ROMANS 5:6–8

Miserable one that I am! Who will deliver me from this mortal body! Thanks be to God through Jesus Christ our Lord. ROMANS 7:24–25a

Hence, now there is no condemnation for those who are in Christ Jesus. For the law of the spirit of life in Christ Jesus has freed you from the law of sin and death. For what the law, weakened by the flesh, was powerless to do, this God has done: by sending his own Son in the likeness of sinful flesh and for the sake of sin, he condemned sin in the flesh, so that the righteous decree of the law might be fulfilled in us, who live not according to the flesh but according to the spirit. ROMANS 8:1–4

We know that all things work for good for those who love God, who are called according to his purpose. For those he foreknew he also predestined to be conformed to the image of his Son, so that he might be the firstborn among many brothers. And those he predestined he also called; and those he called he also justified; and those he justified he also glorified.

ROMANS 8:28–30

What then shall we say to this? If God is for us, who can be against us? He who did not spare his own Son but handed him over for us all, how will he not also give us everything else along with him? Who will bring a charge against God's chosen ones? It is God who acquits us. Who will condemn? It is Christ [Jesus] who died, rather, was raised, who also is at the right hand of God, who indeed intercedes for us. What will separate us from the love of Christ? Will anguish, or distress, or persecution, or famine, or nakedness, or peril, or the sword? As it is written:

"For your sake we are being slain all the day;
We are looked upon as sheep to be slaughtered."
No, in all these things we conquer overwhelmingly through him who loved us. For I am convinced that neither death, nor life, nor angels, nor principalities, nor present things, nor future things, nor powers, nor height, nor depth, nor any other creature will be able to separate us from the love of God in Christ Jesus our Lord. ROMANS 8:31–39

Brothers, my heart's desire and prayer to God on their behalf is for salvation. I testify with regard to them that they have zeal for God, but it is not discerning. For, in their unawareness of the righteousness that comes from God and their attempt to establish their own [righteousness], they did not submit to the righteousness of God. For Christ is the end of the law for the justification of everyone who has faith. ROMANS 10:1–4

But the righteousness that comes from faith says, "Do not say in your heart, 'Who will go up into heaven?' (that is, to bring Christ down) or 'who will go down into the abyss?' (that is, to bring Christ up from the dead)." But what does it say?

"The word is near you,
    in your mouth and in your heart"
(that is, the word of faith that we preach), for, if you confess with your mouth that Jesus is Lord and believe in your heart that God raised him from the dead, you will be saved. For one believes with the heart and so is justified, and one confesses with the mouth and so is saved. For the scripture says, "No one who believes in him will be put to shame." For there is no distinction between Jew and Greek; the same Lord is Lord for all, enriching all who call upon him. For "everyone who calls on the name of the Lord will be saved." ROMANS 10:6–13

"God has overlooked the times of ignorance, but now he demands that all people everywhere repent because he has established a day on which he will 'judge the world with justice' through a man he has appointed, and he has provided confirmation for all by raising him from the dead." ACTS 17:30–31

For Christ did not enter into a sanctuary made by hands, a copy of the true one, but heaven itself, that he might now appear before God on our behalf. Not that he might offer himself repeatedly, as the high priest enters each year into the sanctuary with blood that is not his own; if that were so, he would have had to suffer repeatedly from the foundation of the world. But now once for all he has appeared at the end of the ages to take away sin by his sacrifice. Just as it is appointed that human beings die once, and after this the judgment, so also Christ, offered once to take away the sins of many, will appear a second time, not to take away sin but to bring salvation to those who eagerly await him. HEBREWS 9:24–28

Blessed be the God and Father of our Lord Jesus Christ, who in his great mercy gave us a new birth to a living hope through the resurrection of Jesus Christ from the dead, to an inheritance that is imperishable, undefiled, and unfading, kept in heaven for you who by the power of God are safeguarded through faith, to a salvation that is ready to be revealed in the final time. 1 PETER 1:3–5

He saved us and called us to a holy life, not according to our works but according to his own design and the grace bestowed on us in Christ Jesus before time began, but now made manifest through the appearance of our saviour Christ Jesus, who destroyed death and brought life and immortality to light through the gospel, for which I was appointed preacher and apostle and teacher. 2 TIMOTHY 1:9–11

But when the kindness and generous love
    of God our saviour appeared,
not because of any righteous deeds we had done
    but because of his mercy,

he saved us through the bath of rebirth
   and renewal by the holy Spirit,
whom he richly poured out on us
   through Jesus Christ our saviour,
so that we might be justified by his grace
   and become heirs in hope of eternal life.

TITUS 3:4–7

We know that we belong to God, and the whole world is under the power of the evil one. We also know that the Son of God has come and has given us discernment to know the one who is true. And we are in the one who is true, in his Son Jesus Christ. He is the true God and eternal life. Children, be on your guard against idols. 1 JOHN 5:19–21

"Amen, amen, I say to you, the hour is coming and is now here when the dead will hear the voice of the Son of God, and those who hear will live. For just as the Father has life in himself, so also he gave to his Son the possession of life in himself. And he gave him power to exercise judgment, because he is the Son of Man. Do not be amazed at this, because the hour is coming in which all who are in the tombs will hear his voice and will come out, those who have done good deeds to the resurrection of life, but those who have done wicked deeds to the resurrection of condemnation." JOHN 5:25–29

And do this because you know the time; it is the hour now for you to awake from sleep. For our salvation is nearer now than when we first believed; the night is advanced, the day is at hand. Let us then throw off the works of darkness [and] put on the armour of light; let us conduct ourselves properly as in the day, not in orgies and drunkenness, not in promiscuity and licentiousness, not in rivalry and jealousy. But put on the Lord Jesus Christ, and make no provision for the desire of the flesh. ROMANS 13:11–14

We, who are Jews by nature and not sinners from among the Gentiles, [yet] who know that a person is not justified by works of the law but through faith in Jesus Christ, even we have believed in Christ Jesus that we may be justified by faith in Christ and not by works of the law, because by works of the law no one will be justified. GALATIANS 2:15–16

. . . he destined us for adoption to himself through Jesus Christ, in accord with the favour of his will, for the praise of the glory of his grace that he granted us in the beloved. EPHESIANS 1:5–6

For by grace you have been saved through faith, and this is not from you; it is the gift of God; it is not from works, so no one may boast. For we are his handiwork, created in Christ Jesus for the good works that God has prepared in advance, that we should live in them. EPHESIANS 2:8–10

For God did not send his Son into the world to condemn the world, but that the world might be saved through him. JOHN 3:17

We also know that the Son of God has come and has given us discernment to know the one who is true.

And we are in the one who is true, in his Son Jesus Christ. He is the true God and eternal life.

1 JOHN 5:20

"On the contrary, we believe that we are saved through the grace of the Lord Jesus, in the same way as they." ACTS 15:11

They are justified freely by his grace through the redemption in Christ Jesus, whom God set forth as an expiation, through faith, by his blood, to prove his righteousness because of the forgiveness of sins previously committed, . . . ROMANS 3:24–25

So Jesus said again, "Amen, amen, I say to you, I am the gate for the sheep. All who came [before me] are thieves and robbers, but the sheep did not listen to them. I am the gate. Whoever enters through me will be saved, and will come in and go out and find pasture . . . I am the good shepherd. A good shepherd lays down his life for the sheep." JOHN 10:7–9, 11

But we ought to give thanks to God for you always, brothers loved by the Lord, because God chose you as the first fruits for salvation through sanctification by the Spirit and belief in truth. To this end he has [also] called you through our gospel to possess the glory of our Lord Jesus Christ.

2 THESSALONIANS 2:13–14

Indeed, the grace of our Lord has been abundant, along with the faith and love that are in Christ Jesus.

This saying is trustworthy and deserves full acceptance: Christ Jesus came into the world to save sinners. Of these I am the foremost. 1 TIMOTHY 1:14–15

This is good and pleasing to God our saviour, who
    wills everyone to be saved and to come to
    knowledge of the truth.
For there is one God.
There is also one mediator between God and the
    human race,
Christ Jesus, himself human,
who gave himself as ransom for all.
This was the testimony at the proper time.
                     1 TIMOTHY 2:3–6

8

Faith

Moses writes about the righteousness that comes from [the] law, "The one who does these things will live by them." But the righteousness that comes from faith says, "Do not say in your heart, 'Who will go up into heaven?' (that is, to bring Christ down) or 'Who will go down into the abyss?' (that is, to bring Christ up from the dead)." But what does it say?

"The word is near you,
  in your mouth and in your heart"
(that is, the word of faith that we preach), for, if you confess with your mouth that Jesus is Lord and believe in your heart that God raised him from the dead, you will be saved. For one believes with the heart and so is justified, and one confesses with the mouth and so is saved. For the scripture says, 'No one who believes in him will be put to shame." For there is no distinction between Jew and Greek; the same Lord is Lord of all, enriching all who call upon him. For "everyone who calls on the name of the Lord will be saved." ROMANS 10:5–13

Before faith came, we were held in custody under law, confined for the faith that was to be revealed. Consequently, the law was our disciplinarian for Christ that we might be justified by faith. But now that faith has come, we are no longer under a disciplinarian. For through faith you are all children of God

61

in Christ Jesus. For all of you who were baptized into Christ have clothed yourselves with Christ.

GALATIANS 3:23–27

It is I, Paul, who am telling you that if you have yourselves circumcised, Christ will be of no benefit to you. Once again I declare to every man who has himself circumcised that he is bound to observe the entire law. You are separated from Christ, you who are trying to be justified by law; you have fallen from grace. For through the Spirit, by faith, we await the hope of righteousness. For in Christ Jesus, neither circumcision nor uncircumcision counts for anything, but only faith working through love.

GALATIANS 5:2–6

For by grace you have been saved through faith, and this is not from you; it is the gift of God; it is not from works, so no one may boast. EPHESIANS 2:8–9

And they said, "Believe in the Lord Jesus and you and your household will be saved." ACTS 16:31

But without faith it is impossible to please him, for anyone who approaches God must believe that he exists and that he rewards those who seek him.

HEBREWS 11:6

Everyone who believes that Jesus is the Christ is begotten by God, and everyone who loves the father loves [also] the one begotten by him. In this way we know that we love the children of God when we love

God and obey his commandments. And his commandments are not burdensome, for whoever is begotten
by God conquers the world. And the victory that
conquers the world is our faith. Who [indeed] is the
victor over the world but the one who believes that
Jesus is the Son of God? 1 JOHN 5:1–5

"Whoever believes and is baptized will be saved;
whoever does not believe will be condemned."

MARK 16:16

Thus faith comes from what is heard, and what is
heard comes through the word of Christ.

ROMANS 10:17

Jesus told her, "I am the resurrection and the life;
whoever believes in me, even if he dies, will live, and
everyone who lives and believes in me will never die."

JOHN 11:25–26a

But you, remain faithful to what you have learned and
believed, because you know from whom you learned
it, . . . 2 TIMOTHY 3:14

Take care, brothers, that none of you may have an
evil and unfaithful heart, so as to forsake the living
God. Encourage yourselves daily while it is still
"today," so that none of you may grow hardened by
the deceit of sin. HEBREWS 3:12–13

Therefore, do not throw away your confidence; it will
have great recompense. You need endurance to do the
will of God and receive what he has promised.

"For, after just a brief moment,
he who is to come shall come;
he shall not delay.
But my just one shall live by faith,
and if he draws back I take no pleasure in him."
We are not among those who draw back and perish,
but among those who have faith and will possess life.

HEBREWS 10:35–39

Faith is the realization of what is hoped for and evidence of things not seen. Because of it the ancients were well attested . . . But without faith it is impossible to please him, for anyone who approaches God must believe that he exists and that he rewards those who seek him. HEBREWS 11:1–2, 6

In this you rejoice, although now for a little while you may have to suffer through various trials, so that the genuineness of your faith, more precious than gold that is perishable even though tested by fire, may prove to be for praise, glory, and honour at the revelation of Jesus Christ. Although you have not seen him you love him; even though you do not see him now yet believe in him, you rejoice with an indescribable and glorious joy, as you attain the goal of [your] faith, the salvation of your souls. 1 PETER 1:6–9

For this very reason, make every effort to supplement your faith with virtue, virtue with knowledge, knowledge with self-control, self-control with endurance, endurance with devotion, devotion with mutual affection, mutual affection with love. If these are yours and increase in abundance, they will keep you from being idle or unfruitful in the knowledge of our Lord Jesus Christ. 2 PETER 1:5–8

Whoever believes in the Son of God has this testimony within himself. Whoever does not believe God has made him a liar by not believing the testimony God has given about his Son. And this is the testimony: God gave us eternal life, and this life is in his Son. Whoever possesses the Son has life; whoever does not possess the Son of God does not have life.

1 JOHN 5:10–12

But you, beloved, build yourselves up in your most holy faith; pray in the holy Spirit. Keep yourselves in the love of God and wait for the mercy of our Lord Jesus Christ that leads to eternal life. JUDE 20–21

"Believe me that I am in the Father and the Father is in me, or else, believe because of the works themselves. Amen, amen, I say to you, whoever believes in me will do the works that I do, and will do greater ones than these, because I am going to the Father. And whatever you ask in my name, I will do, so that the Father may be glorified in the Son. If you ask anything of me in my name, I will do it."

JOHN 14:11–14

III

God and Our Personal Needs

9

Guidance and Direction

"Above all, be firm and steadfast, taking care to observe the entire law which my servant Moses enjoined on you. Do not swerve from it either to the right or to the left, that you may succeed wherever you go. Keep this book of the law on your lips. Recite it by day and by night, that you may observe carefully all that is written in it; then you will successfully attain your goal. I command you: be firm and steadfast! Do not fear nor be dismayed, for the LORD, your God, is with you wherever you go." JOSHUA 1:7–9

You indeed, O LORD, give light to my lamp;
   O my God, you brighten the darkness about
      me; . . . PSALM 18:29

Yet with you I shall always be;
   you have hold of my right hand;
With your counsel you guide me,
   and in the end you will receive me in glory.
               PSALM 73:23–24

The LORD is God, and he has given us light.
               PSALM 118:27a

A lamp to my feet is your word,
   a light to my path. PSALM 119:105

The revelation of your words sheds light,
    giving understanding to the simple. PSALM 119:130

"Do not take gold or silver or copper for your belts;
no sack for the journey, or a second tunic, or sandals,
or walking stick. The labourer deserves his keep.
Whatever town or village you enter, look for a worthy
person in it, and stay there until you leave. As you
enter a house, wish it peace. If the house is worthy,
let your peace come upon it; if not, let your peace
return to you. Whoever will not receive you or listen
to your words – go outside that house or town and
shake the dust from your feet. Amen, I say to you, it
will be more tolerable for the land of Sodom and
Gomorrah on the day of judgment than for that town.

"Behold, I am sending you like sheep in the midst
of wolves; so be shrewd as serpents and simple as
doves. But beware of people, for they will hand you
over to courts and scourge you in their synagogues,
and you will be led before governors and kings for my
sake as a witness before them and the pagans. When
they hand you over, do not worry about how you are
to speak or what you are to say. You will be given at
that moment what you are to say. For it will not be
you who speak but the Spirit of your Father speaking
through you." MATTHEW 10:9–20

"But when he comes, the Spirit of truth, he will guide
you to all truth. He will not speak on his own, but he
will speak what he hears, and will declare to you the
things that are coming." JOHN 16:13

"See, I am sending an angel before you, to guard you on the way and bring you to the place I have prepared. Be attentive to him and heed his voice."

EXODUS 23:20–21

"I myself," the LORD answered, "will go along, to give you rest." EXODUS 33:14

Yet there too you shall seek the LORD, your God; and you shall indeed find him when you search after him with your whole heart and your whole soul.

DEUTERONOMY 4:29

I will instruct you to show you the way you should
    walk;
  I will counsel you, keeping my eye on you.

PSALM 32:8

"And I will ask the Father, and he will give you another Advocate to be with you always, . . . I will not leave you orphans; I will come to you."

JOHN 14:16, 18

I will lead the blind on their journey;
  by paths unknown I will guide them.
I will turn darkness into light before them,
  and make crooked ways straight.
These things I will do for them,
  and I will not forsake them ISAIAH 42:16

For I know well the plans I have in mind for you, says the LORD, plans for your welfare, not for woe! plans to give you a future full of hope. When you call me,

when you go to pray for me, I will listen to you. When
you look for me, you will find me. Yes, when you seek
me with all your heart, you will find me with you, says
the LORD, and I will change your lot; I will gather you
together from all the nations and all the places to which
I have banished you, says the LORD, and bring you back
to the place from which I have exiled you.

JEREMIAH 29:11–15

"I have much more to tell you, but you cannot bear
it now. But when he comes, the Spirit of truth, he
will guide you to all truth. He will not speak on his
own, but he will speak what he hears, and will declare
to you the things that are coming." JOHN 16:12–13

"Consecrate them in the truth. Your word is truth. As
you sent me into the world, so I sent them into the
world. And I consecrate myself for them, so that they
also may be consecrated in truth." JOHN 17:17–19

In the same way, the Spirit too comes to the aid of
our weakness; for we do not know how to pray as we
ought, but the Spirit itself intercedes with inexpressi-
ble groanings. And the one who searches hearts knows
what is the intention of the Spirit, because it
intercedes for the holy ones according to God's will.

ROMANS 8:26–27

By the LORD are the steps of a man made firm,
   and he approves his way. PSALM 37:23

For God did not give us a spirit of cowardice but
rather of power and love and self-control.

2 TIMOTHY 1:7

. . . that such is God,
Our God forever and ever;
   he will guide us. PSALM 48:15

. . . With your counsel you guide me,
and in the end you will receive me in glory.
                         PSALM 73:24

O God, when you went forth at the head of your
    people,
   when you marched through the wilderness,
The earth quaked; it rained from heaven at the
    presence of God,
   at the presence of God, the God of Israel, the One
    of Sinai. PSALM 68:8–9

My sheep hear my voice; I know them, and they follow
me. I give them eternal life, and they shall never
perish. No one can take them out of my hand. My
Father, who has given them to me, is greater than all,
and no one can take them out of the Father's hand.
                         JOHN 10:27–29

Thomas said to him, "Master, we do not know where
you are going; how can we know the way?" Jesus said
to him, "I am the way and the truth and the life. No
one comes to the Father except through me. If you
know me, then you will also know my Father. From
now on you do know him and have seen him."
                         JOHN 14:5–7

"My son, forget not my teaching,
  keep in mind my commands;

For many days, and years of life,
    and peace, will they bring you.
Let not kindness and fidelity leave you;
    bind them around your neck;
Then will you win favour and good esteem
    before God and man.
Trust in the LORD with all your heart,
    on your own intelligence rely not;
In all your ways be mindful of him,
    and he will make straight your paths.
Be not wise in your own eyes,
    fear the LORD and turn away from evil;
This will mean health for your flesh
    and vigor for your bones." PROVERBS 3:1–8

Hear, O children, a father's instruction,
    be attentive, that you may gain understanding!
Yes, excellent advice I give you;
    my teaching do not forsake.
When I was my father's child,
    frail, yet the darling of my mother,
He taught me, and said to me:
    "Let your heart hold fast my words:
    keep my commands, that you may live!"
                PROVERBS 4:1–4

Hear, my son, and receive my words,
    and the years of your life shall be many.
On the way of wisdom I direct you,
I lead you on straightforward paths.
When you walk, your step will not be impeded,
    and should you run, you will not stumble.
Hold fast to instruction, never let her go;
    keep her, for she is your life. PROVERBS 4:10–13

10

Courage and Encouragement

For I am convinced that neither death, nor life, nor angels, nor principalities, nor present things, nor future things, nor powers, nor height, nor depth, nor any other creature will be able to separate us from the love of God in Christ Jesus our Lord.

ROMANS 8:38–39

I lift up my eyes toward the mountains;
    whence shall help come to me?
My help is from the LORD,
    who made heaven and earth.
May he not suffer your foot to slip;
    may he slumber not who guards you:
Indeed he neither slumbers nor sleeps,
    the guardian of Israel.
The LORD is your guardian; the LORD is your shade;
    he is beside you at your right hand.
The sun shall not harm you by day,
    nor the moon by night.
The LORD will guard you from all evil;
    he will guard your life.
The LORD will guard your coming and your going,
    both now and forever. PSALM 121

Therefore, brothers, be all the more eager to make your call and election firm, for, in doing so, you will never stumble. 2 PETER 1:10

I heard a loud voice from the throne saying, "Behold, God's dwelling is with the human race. He will dwell with them and they will be his people and God himself will always be with them [as their God]."

REVELATION 21:3

The LORD said to him, "Who gives one man speech and makes another deaf and dumb? Or who gives sight to one and makes another blind? Is it not I, the LORD? Go, then! It is I who will assist you in speaking and will teach you what you are to say."

EXODUS 4:11–12

But Moses answered the people, "Fear not! Stand your ground, and you will see the victory the LORD will win for you today . . . The LORD himself will fight for you; you have only to keep still."

EXODUS 14:13a–14

Blessed be the God and Father of our Lord Jesus Christ, the Father of compassion and God of all encouragement, who encourages us in our every affliction, so that we may be able to encourage those who are in any affliction with the encouragement with which we ourselves are encouraged by God. For as Christ's sufferings overflow to us, so through Christ does our encouragement also overflow. If we are afflicted, it is for your encouragement and salvation; if we are encouraged, it is for your encouragement, which enables you to endure the same sufferings that we suffer. Our hope for you is firm, for we know that as you share in the sufferings, you also share in the encouragement. 2 CORINTHIANS 1:3–7

So we are always courageous, although we know that while we are at home in the body we are away from the Lord, for we walk by faith, not by sight. Yet we are courageous, and we would rather leave the body and go home to the Lord. 2 CORINTHIANS 5:6–8

Rejoice in the Lord always. I shall say it again: rejoice! Your kindness should be known to all. The Lord is near. Have no anxiety at all, but in everything, by prayer and petition, with thanksgiving, make your requests known to God. Then the peace of God that surpasses all understanding will guard your hearts and minds in Christ Jesus. PHILIPPIANS 4:4–7

"I command you: be firm and steadfast! Do not fear nor be dismayed, for the LORD, your God, is with you wherever you go." JOSHUA 1:9

Some are strong in chariots; some, in horses:
    but we are strong in the name of the LORD, our
      God.
Though they bow down and fall,
    yet we stand erect and firm. PSALM 20:8–9

The LORD is my light and my salvation;
    whom should I fear?
The LORD is my life's refuge;
    of whom should I be afraid?
When evildoers come to me
    to devour my flesh,
My foes and my enemies
    themselves stumble and fall.
Though an army encamp against me,

my heart will not fear;
Though war be waged upon me,
    even then will I trust . . .
For he will hide me in his abode
    in the day of trouble;
He will conceal me in the shelter of his tent,
    he will set me high upon a rock. PSALM 27:1–3, 5

. . . the LORD is my strength and my shield.
In him my heart trusts, and I find help;
    then my heart exults, and with my song I give him
        thanks. PSALM 28:7

The LORD is the strength of his people,
    the saving refuge of his anointed. PSALM 28:8

I sought the LORD, and he answered me
    and delivered me from all my fears.
Look to him that you may be radiant with joy,
    and your faces may not flush with shame.
                        PSALM 34:5–6

You shall not fear the terror of the night
    nor the arrow that flies by day;
Not the pestilence that roams in darkness
    nor the devastating plague at noon.
Though a thousand fall at your side,
    ten thousand at your right side,
    near you it shall not come.
Rather with your eyes shall you behold
    and see the requital of the wicked,
Because you have the LORD for your stronghold.
No evil shall befall you,

nor shall affliction come near your tent,
For to his angels he has given command about you,
  that they guard you in all your ways.
                    PSALM 91:5–11

In my straits I called upon the LORD;
  the LORD answered me and set me free.
The LORD is with me; I fear not;
  what can man do against me?
The LORD is with me to help me,
  and I shall look down upon my foes.
It is better to take refuge in the LORD
  than to trust in man . . .
My strength and my courage is the LORD,
  and he has been my saviour. PSALM 118:5–8, 14

Be not afraid of sudden terror,
  of the ruin of the wicked when it comes;
For the LORD will be your confidence,
  and will keep your foot from the snare.
                    PROVERBS 3:25–26

God indeed is my saviour,
  I am confident and unafraid.
My strength and my courage is the LORD,
  and he has been my saviour.
With joy you will draw water
  at the fountain of salvation, . . . ISAIAH 12:2–3a

Do you not know
  or have you not heard?
The LORD is the eternal God,
  creator of the ends of the earth.

He does not faint nor grow weary,
  and his knowledge is beyond scrutiny.
He gives strength to the fainting;
  for the weak he makes vigour abound.
Though young men faint and grow weary,
  and youths stagger and fall,
They that hope in the LORD will renew their
    strength,
  they will soar as with eagles' wings;
They will run and not grow weary,
  walk and not grow faint. ISAIAH 40:28–31

For I am the LORD, your God,
  who grasp your right hand;
It is I who say to you, "Fear not,
  I will help you."
Fear not, O worm Jacob,
  O maggot Israel;
I will help you, says the LORD;
  your redeemer is the Holy One of Israel.
                    ISAIAH 41:13–14

O LORD, you are my God,
  I will extol you and praise your name;
For you have fulfilled your wonderful plans of old,
  faithful and true.
For you have made the city a heap,
  the fortified city a ruin;
The castle of the insolent is a city no more,
  nor ever to be rebuilt.
Therfore a strong people will honour you,
  fierce nations will fear you.
For you are a refuge to the poor,
  a refuge to the needy in distress;

Shelter from the rain,
　　shade from the heat.
As with the cold rain,
　　as with the desert heat,
　　even so you quell the uproar of the wanton.
On this mountain the LORD of hosts
　　will provide for all peoples
A feast of rich food and choice wines,
　　juicy, rich food and pure, choice wines.
On this mountain he will destroy
　　the veil that veils all peoples,
The web that is woven over all nations;
　　he will destroy death forever.
The Lord God will wipe away
　　the tears from all faces;
The reproach of his people he will remove
　　from the whole earth; for the LORD has spoken.
　　On that day it will be said:
"Behold our God, to whom we looked to save us!
　　This is the LORD for whom we looked;
　　let us rejoice and be glad that he has saved us!"
ISAIAH 25:1–9

　　On that day they will sing this song in the land of
　　　　Judah:
"A strong city have we;
　　he sets up walls and ramparts to protect us.
Open up the gates
　　to let in a nation that is just,
　　one that keeps faith.
A nation of firm purpose you keep in peace;
　　in peace, for its trust in you."

Trust in the LORD forever!
  For the LORD is an eternal Rock. ISAIAH 26:1–4

Strengthen the hands that are feeble,
  make firm the knees that are weak,
Say to those whose hearts are frightened:
  be strong, fear not!
Here is your God,
  he comes with vindication;
With divine recompense
  he comes to save you.
Then will the eyes of the blind be opened,
  the ears of the deaf be cleared;
then will the lame leap like a stag,
  then the tongue of the dumb will sing.
                    ISAIAH 35:3–6

Comfort, give comfort to my people,
  says your God.
Speak tenderly to Jerusalem, and proclaim to her
  that her service is at an end,
    her guilt is expiated;
Indeed, she has received from the hand of the LORD
  double for all her sins. ISAIAH 40:1–2

Go up onto a high mountain,
  Zion, herald of glad tidings;
Cry out at the top of your voice,
  Jerusalem, herald of good news!
Fear not to cry out
  and say to the cities of Judah;
    Here is your God!
Here comes with power

the Lord God,
  who rules by his strong arm;
Here is his reward with him,
  his recompense before him.
Like a shepherd he feeds his flock;
  in his arms he gathers the lambs,
Carrying them in his bosom,
  and leading the ewes with care. ISAIAH 40:9–11

But now, thus says the LORD,
  who created you, O Jacob, and formed you, O
    Israel:
Fear not, for I have redeemed you;
  I have called you by name: you are mine.
When you pass through the water, I will be with you;
  in the rivers you shall not drown.
When you walk through fire, you shall not be
    burned;
  the flames shall not consume you.
For I am the LORD, your God,
  the Holy One of Israel, your saviour.
I give Egypt as your ransom,
  Ethiopia and Seba in return for you.
Because you are precious in my eyes
  and glorious, and because I love you.
I give men in return for you
  and peoples in exchange for your life.
Fear not, for I am with you;
  from the east I will bring back your descendants,
  from the west I will gather you.
I will say to the north: Give them up!
  and to the south: Hold not back!
Bring back my sons from afar,

and my daughters from the ends of the earth:
Everyone who is named as mine,
   whom I created for my glory,
   whom I formed and made. ISAIAH 43:1–7

The LORD calls you back,
   like a wife forsaken and grieved in spirit,
A wife married in youth and then cast off,
   says your God.
For a brief moment I abandoned you,
   but with great tenderness I will take you back.
In an outburst of wrath, for a moment
   I hid my face from you;
But with enduring love I take pity on you,
   says the LORD, your redeemer.
This is for me like the days of Noah,
   when I swore that the waters of Noah
   should never again deluge the earth;
So I have sworn not to be angry with you,
   or to rebuke you.
Though the mountains leave their place
   and the hills be shaken,
My love shall never leave you
   nor my covenant of peace be shaken,
   says the LORD, who has mercy on you.
               ISAIAH 54:6–10

Behold, I will treat and assuage the city's wounds;
I will heal them, and reveal to them an abundance of
lasting peace. I will change the lot of Judah and the
lot of Israel, and rebuild them as of old. I will cleanse
them of all the guilt they incurred by sinning against
me; all their offences by which they sinned and

rebelled against me, I will forgive. Then Jerusalem shall be my joy, my praise, my glory, before all the nations of the earth, as they hear of all the good I will do among them. They shall be in fear and trembling over all the peaceful benefits I will give her.

JEREMIAH 33:6–9

You shall be my people,
   and I will be your God. JEREMIAH 30:22

Therefore, do not throw away your confidence; it will have great recompense. You need endurance to do the will of God and receive what he has promised.

HEBREWS 10:35–36

Let us not grow tired of doing good, for in due time we shall reap our harvest, if we do not give up.

GALATIANS 6:9

"Come, let us return to the LORD,
For it is he who has rent, but he will heal us;
   he has struck us, but he will bind our wounds.
He will revive us after two days;
   on the third day he will raise us up,
   to live in his presence.
Let us know, let us strive to know the LORD;
   as certain as the dawn is his coming,
   and his judgment shines forth like the light of day!
He will come to us like the rain,
   like spring rain that waters the earth."

HOSEA 6:1–3

Fear not, O land!
  exult and rejoice!
  for the LORD has done great things.
Fear not, beasts of the field!
  for the pastures of the plain are green;
The tree bears its fruit,
  the fig tree and the vine give their yield.
And do you, O children of Zion, exult
  and rejoice in the LORD, your God!
He has given you the teacher of justice;
  he has made the rain come down for you,
  the early and the late rain as before.
The threshing floors shall be full of grain
  and the vats shall overflow with wine and oil.
And I will repay you for the years
  which the locust has eaten,
The grasshopper, the devourer, and the cutter,
  my great army which I sent among you.
You shall eat and be filled,
  and shall praise the name of the LORD, your God,
Because he has dealt wondrously with you;
  my people shall nevermore be put to shame.
And you shall know that I am in the midst of Israel;
  I am the LORD, your God, and there is no other;
  my people shall nevermore be put to shame.

JOEL 2:21–27

On that day, it shall be said to Jerusalem:
  Fear not, O Zion, be not discouraged!
The LORD, your God, is in your midst,
  a mighty saviour;
He will rejoice over you with gladness,
  and renew you in his love.

He will sing joyfully because of you,
  as one sings at festivals.
I will remove disaster from among you,
  so that none may recount your disgrace.
Yes, at that time I will deal
  with all who oppress you:
I will save the lame,
  and assemble the outcasts;
I will give them praise and renown
  in all the earth, when I bring about their
    restoration.
At that time I will bring you home,
  and at that time I will gather you;
For I will give you renown and praise,
  among all the peoples of the earth,
When I bring about your restoration
  before your very eyes, says the LORD
              ZEPHANIAH 3:16–20

I am confident of this, that the one who began a good work in you will continue to complete it until the day of Christ Jesus. PHILIPPIANS 1:6

"Ask and it will be given to you; seek and you will find; knock and the door will be opened to you. For everyone who asks, receives; and the one who seeks, finds; and to the one who knocks, the door will be opened. Which one of you would hand his son a stone when he asks for a loaf of bread, or a snake when he asks for a fish? If you then, who are wicked, know how to give good gifts to your children, how much more will your heavenly Father give good things to those who ask him." MATTHEW 7:7–11

"Behold, I am sending you like sheep in the midst of wolves; so be shrewd as serpents and simple as doves. But beware of people, for they will hand you over to courts and scourge you in their synagogues, and you will be led before governors and kings for my sake as a witness before them and the pagans. When they hand you over, do not worry about how you are to speak or what you are to say. You will be given at that moment what you are to say. For it will not be you who speak but the Spirit of your Father speaking through you. Brother will hand over brother to death, and the father his child; children will rise up against parents and have them put to death. You will be hated by all because of my name, but whoever endures to the end will be saved. When they persecute you in one town, flee to another. Amen, I say to you, you will not finish the towns of Israel before the Son of Man comes . . .

"Therefore do not be afraid of them. Nothing is concealed that will not be revealed, nor secret that will not be known. What I say to you in the darkness, speak in the light; what you hear whispered, proclaim on the housetops. And do not be afraid of those who kill the body but cannot kill the soul; rather, be afraid of the one who destroy both soul and body in Gehenna. Are not two sparrows sold for a small coin? Yet not one of them falls to the ground without your Father's knowledge. Even all the hairs of your head are counted. So do not be afraid; you are worth more than many sparrows." MATTHEW 10:16–23, 26–31

But the Lord is faithful; he will strengthen you and guard you from the evil one. 2 THESSALONIANS 3:3

We know that no one begotten by God sins; but the one begotten by God he protects, and the evil one cannot touch him. 1 JOHN 5:18

"I have told you this so that you might have peace in me. In the world you will have trouble, but take courage, I have conquered the world." JOHN 16:33

We urge you, brothers, admonish the idle, cheer the fainthearted, support the weak, be patient with all. 1 THESSALONIANS 5:14

Be on your guard, stand firm in the faith, be courageous, be strong. Your every act should be done with love. 1 CORINTHIANS 16:13–14

11

Trial and Temptation

"So while we wait for the salvation that comes from him, let us call upon him to help us, and he will hear our cry if it is his good pleasure." JUDITH 8:17

"Besides all this, we should be grateful to the LORD our God, for putting us to the test, as he did our forefathers. Recall how he dealt with Abraham, and how he tried Isaac, and all that happened to Jacob in Syrian Mesopotamia while he was tending the flocks of Laban, his mother's brother. Not for vengeance did the LORD put them in the crucible to try their hearts, nor has he done so with us. It is by way of admonition that he chastises those who are close to him."

JUDITH 8:25–27

Happy is the man whom God reproves!
  The Almighty's chastening do not reject.
For he wounds, but he binds up;
  he smites, but his hands give healing. JOB 5:17–18

For his anger lasts but a moment;
  a lifetime, his good will.
At nightfall, weeping enters in,
  but with the dawn, rejoicing. PSALM 30:6

No trial has come to you but what is human. God is faithful and will not let you be tried beyond your strength; but with the trial he will provide a way out, so that you may be able to bear it. 1 CORINTHIANS 10:13

Behold, God will not cast away the upright;
  neither will he take the hand of the wicked.
Once more will he fill your mouth with laughter,
  and your lips with rejoicing. JOB 8:20–21

You do see, for you behold misery and sorrow,
  taking them in your hands.
On you the unfortunate man depends;
  of the fatherless you are the helper . . .
The desire of the afflicted you, hear, O LORD;
  strengthening their hearts, you pay heed
to the defence of the fatherless and the oppressed,
  that man, who is of earth, may terrify no more.
                    PSALM 10:14, 17–18

The LORD is close to the brokenhearted;
  and those who are crushed in spirit he saves.
                    PSALM 34–19

Those that sow in tears
  shall reap rejoicing.
Although they go forth weeping,
  carrying the seed to be sown,
They shall come back rejoicing,
  carrying their sheaves. PSALM 126:5–6

But the souls of the just are in the hand of God,
  and no torment shall touch them.

They seemed, in the view of the foolish, to be dead;
  and their passing away was thought an affliction
  and their going forth from us, utter destruction.
But they are in peace.
For if before men, indeed, they be punished,
  yet is their hope full of immortality;
Chastised a little, they shall be greatly blessed,
  because God tried them
  and found them worthy of himself.
As gold in the furnace, he proved them,
  and as sacrificial offerings he took them to himself.
In the time of their visitation they shall shine,
  and shall dart about as sparks through stubble;
They shall judge nations and rule over peoples,
  and the LORD shall be their King forever.
                              WISDOM 3:1–8

"Give us today our daily bread;
and forgive us our debts,
as we forgive our debtors;
and do not subject us to the final test,
  but deliver us from the evil one."
                              MATTHEW 6:11–13

Because he himself was tested through what he suffered, he is able to help those who are being tested.
                              HEBREWS 2:18

Consider it all joy, my brothers, when you encounter various trials, for you know that the testing of your faith produces perseverance. JAMES 1:2–3

Finally, draw your strength from the Lord and from his mighty power. Put on the armour of God so that you may be able to stand firm against the tactics of the devil. For our struggle is not with flesh and blood but with powers, with the world rulers of this present darkness, with the evil spirits in the heavens. Therefore, put on the armour of God, that you may be able to resist on the evil day and, having done everything, to hold your ground. So stand fast with your loins girded in truths, clothed with righteousness as a breastplate, and your feet shod in readiness for the gospel of peace. In all circumstances, hold faith as a shield, to quench all [the] flaming arrows of the evil one. And take the helmet of salvation and the sword of the Spirit, which is the word of God.

With all prayer and supplication, pray at every opportunity in the Spirit. To that end, be watchful with all perseverance and supplication for all the holy ones . . . EPHESIANS 6:10–18

Blessed is the man who perseveres in temptation, for when he has been proved he will receive the crown of life that he promised to those who love him. No one experiencing temptation should say, "I am being tempted by God"; for God is not subject to temptation to evil, and he himself tempts no one. Rather, each person is tempted when he is lured and enticed by his own desire. JAMES 1:12–14

So submit yourselves to God. Resist the devil, and he will flee from you. JAMES 4:7

"Simon, Simon, behold Satan has demanded to sift all of you like wheat, but I have prayed that your own faith may not fail; and once you have turned back, you must strengthen your brothers." LUKE 22:31–32

No, in all these things we conquer overwhelmingly through him who loved us. For I am convinced that neither death, nor life, nor angels, nor principalities, nor present things, nor future things, nor powers, nor height, nor depth, nor any other creature will be able to separate us from the love of God in Christ Jesus our Lord. ROMANS 8:37–39

Be sober and vigilant. Your opponent the devil is prowling around like a roaring lion looking for [someone] to devour. Resist him, steadfast in faith, knowing that your fellow believers throughout the world undergo the same sufferings. The God of all grace who called you to his eternal glory through Christ [Jesus] will himself restore, confirm, strengthen, and establish you after you have suffered a little. To him be dominion forever. Amen. 1 PETER 5:8–11

. . . but he said to me, "My grace is sufficient for you, for power is made perfect in weakness." I will rather boast most gladly of my weaknesses, in order that the power of Christ may dwell with me.

2 CORINTHIANS 12:9

. . . for whoever is begotten by God conquers the world. And the victory that conquers the world is our faith. 1 JOHN 5:4

Do not be conquered by evil but conquer evil with good. ROMANS 12:21

Let us hold unwaveringly to our confession that gives us hope, for he who made the promise is trustworthy.
HEBREWS 10:23

"Whoever has ears ought to hear what the Spirit says to the churches. To the victor I will give the right to eat from the tree of life that is in the garden of God." REVELATION 2:7

"I will give the victor the right to sit with me on my throne, as I myself first won the victory and sit with my Father on his throne." REVELATION 3:21

Beloved, do not be surprised that a trial by fire is occurring among you, as if something strange were happening to you. But rejoice to the extent that you share in the sufferings of Christ, so that when his glory is revealed you may also revoice exultantly. If you are insulted for the name of Christ, blessed are you, for the Spirit of glory and of God rests upon you. But let no one among you be made to suffer as a murderer, a thief, an evildoer, or as an intriguer. But whoever is made to suffer as a Christian should not be ashamed but glorify God because of the name. For it is time for the judgment to begin with the household of God; if it begins with us, how will it end for those who fail to obey the gospel of God?
"And if the righteous one is barely saved,
   Where will the godless and the sinner appear?"
As a result, those who suffer in accord with God's will

hand their souls over to a faithful creator as they do good. 1 PETER 4:12–19

In this you rejoice, although now for a little while you may have to suffer through various trials, so that the genuineness of your faith, more precious than gold that is perishable even though tested by fire, may prove to be for praise, glory, and honour at the revelation of Jesus Christ. 1 PETER 1:6–7

12

When in Trouble or Distress

Yet the LORD is waiting to show you favour,
   and he rises to pity you;
For the LORD is a God of justice:
   blessed are all who wait for him!
O people of Zion, who dwell in Jerusalem,
   no more will you weep;
He will be gracious to you when you cry out,
   as soon as he hears he will answer you.
The LORD will give you the bread you need
   and the water for which you thirst.
No longer will your Teacher hide himself,
   but with your own eyes you shall see your
     Teacher,
While from behind, a voice shall sound in your ears:
   "This is the way; walk in it,"
   when you would turn to the right or to the left.
                   ISAIAH 30:18–21

He will give rain for the seed
   that you sow in the ground,
And the wheat that the soul produces
   will be rich and abundant.
On that day your cattle will graze
   in spacious meadows;
The oxen and the asses that till the ground
   will eat silage tossed to them

with shovel and pitchfork.
Upon every high mountain and lofty hill
    there will be streams of running water.
On the day of the great slaughter,
    when the towers fall,
The light of the moon will be like that of the sun
    and the light of the sun will be seven times greater
    [like the light of seven days].
On the day the LORD binds up the wounds of his
      people,
    he will heal the bruises left by his blows.
                    ISAIAH 30:23–26

You have preserved my life
    from the pit of destruction,
When you cast behind your back
    all my sins.
For it is not the nether world that gives you thanks,
    nor death that praises you;
Neither do those who go down into the pit
    await your kindness.
The living, the living give you thanks.
    as I do today.
Fathers declare to their sons,
    O God, your faithfulness.
The LORD is our saviour;
    we shall sing to stringed instruments
In the house of the LORD
    all the days of our life. ISAIAH 38:17b–20

How could I give you up, O Ephraim,
    or deliver you up, O Israel?
How could I treat you as Admah,

or make you like Zeboiim?
My heart is overwhelmed,
    my pity is stirred.
I will not give vent to my blazing anger,
    I will not destroy Ephraim again;
For I am God and not man,
    the Holy One present among you;
        I will not let the flames consume you.
                                    HOSEA 11:8–9

Return, O Israel, to the LORD, your God;
    you have collapsed through your guilt.
Take with you words,
    and return to the LORD;
Say to him, "Forgive all iniquity,
    and receive what is good, that we may render
    as offerings the bullocks from our stalls.
Assyria will not save us,
    nor shall we have horses to mount;
We shall say no more, 'Our god,'
    to the work of our hands;
        for in you the orphan finds compassion."
I will heal their defection,
    I will love them freely;
        for my wrath is turned away from them.
I will be like the dew for Israel:
    he shall blossom like the lily;
He shall strike root like the Lebanon cedar,
    and put forth his shoots.
His spendour shall be like the olive tree
    and his fragrance like the Lebanon cedar.
Again they shall dwell in his shade
    and raise grain;

They shall blossom like the vine,
and his fame shall be like the wine of Lebanon.
HOSEA 14:2–8

Though I walk amid distress, you preserve me;
against the anger of my enemies you raise your
hand;
your right hand saves me. PSALM 138:7

When the afflicted man called out, the LORD heard,
and from all his distress he saved him. PSALM 34:7

You indeed, O LORD, give light to my lamp;
O my God, you brighten the darkness about me;
For with your aid I run against an armed band,
and by the help of my God I leap over a wall.
PSALM 18:29–30

For who is God except the LORD?
Who is a rock, save our God?
The God who girded me with strength
and kept my way unerring;
Who made my feet swift as those of hinds
and set me on the heights;
Who trained my hands for war
and my arms to bend a bow of brass.
You have given me your saving shield;
your right hand has upheld me,
and you have stooped to make me great.
You made room for my steps;
unwavering was my stride.
I pursued my enemies and overtook them,
nor did I turn again till I made an end of them.

I smote them and they could not rise;
    they fell beneath my feet. PSALM 18:32–39

The LORD answer you in time of distress;
    the name of the God of Jacob defend you!
May he send you help from the sanctuary,
    from Zion may be sustain you.
May he remember all your offerings
    and graciously accept your holocaust.
                    PSALM 20:2–4

You are my rock and my fortress;
    for your name's sake you will lead and guide me.
You will free me from the snare they set for me,
    for you are my refuge.
Into your hands I commend my spirit;
    you will redeem me, O LORD, O faithful God.
                    PSALM 31:4–6

For this shall every faithful man pray to you
    in time of stress.
Though deep waters overflow,
    they shall not reach him.
You are my shelter; from distress you will preserve
    me;
    with glad cries of freedom you will ring me round.
                    PSALM 32:6–7

God is our refuge and our strength,
    an ever-present help in distress.
Therefore we fear not, though the earth be shaken
    and mountains plunge into the depths of the sea;
Though its waters rage and foam

and the mountains quake at its surging.
The LORD of hosts is with us;
    our stronghold is the God of Jacob. PSALM 46:2–4

Behold, God is my helper,
    the Lord sustains my life. PSALM 54:4

Cast your care upon the LORD,
    and he will support you;
      never will he permit the just man to be disturbed.
                    PSALM 55:23

Give us aid against the foe,
    for worthless is the help of men.
Under God we shall do valiantly;
    it is he who will tread down our foes.
              PSALM 60:13–14

Only in God be at rest, my soul,
    for from him comes my hope.
He only is my rock and my salvation,
    my stronghold; I shall not be disturbed.
With God is my safety and my glory,
    he is the rock of my strength; my refuge is in God.
Trust in him at all times, O my people!
    pour out your hearts before him;
    God is our refuge! PSALM 62:6–9

The LORD is near to all who call upon him,
    to all who call upon him in truth.
He fulfils the desire of those who fear him,
    he hears their cry and saves them.
The LORD keeps all who love him,

but all the wicked he will destroy.
PSALM 145:18–20

I was at the point of death,
my soul was nearing the depths of the nether
world;
I turned every way, but there was no one to help me,
I looked for one to sustain me, but could find no
one.
But then I remembered the mercies of the LORD,
his kindness through ages past;
For he saves those who take refuge in him,
and rescues them from every evil. SIRACH 51:6b–8

For you are a refuge to the poor,
a refuge to the needy in distress;
Shelter from the rain,
shade from the heat.
As with the cold rain, . . . ISAIAH 25:4

Happy he whose help is the God of Jacob,
whose hope is in the LORD, his God,
Who made heaven and earth,
the sea and all that is in them;
Who keeps faith forever,
secures justice for the oppressed,
gives food to the hungry.
The LORD sets captives free;
the LORD gives sight to the blind.
The LORD raises up those that were bowed down;
the LORD loves the just.
The LORD protects strangers;
the fatherless and the widow he sustains,

but the way of the wicked he thwarts.
PSALM 146:5–9

The LORD is my shepherd; I shall not want.
  In verdant pastures he gives me repose;
Beside restful waters he leads me;
  he refreshes my soul.
He guides me in right paths
  for his name's sake.
Even though I walk in the dark valley
  I fear no evil; for you are at my side
With your rod and your staff
  that give me courage.
You spread the table before me
  in the sight of my foes;
You anoint my head with oil;
  my cup overflows.
Only goodness and kindness follow me
  all the days of my life;
And I shall dwell in the house of the LORD
  for years to come. PSALM 23:1–6

For though the fig tree blossom not
  nor fruit be on the vines,
Though the yield of the olive fail
  and the terraces produce no nourishment.
Though the flocks disappear from the fold
  and there be no herd in the stalls,
Yet will I rejoice in the LORD
  and exult in my saving God. HABAKKUK 3:17–18

What then shall we say to this? If God is for us,
who can be against us? He who did not spare his own

Son but handed him over for us all, how will he not also give us everything else along with him? Who will bring a charge against God's chosen ones? It is God who acquits us. Who will condemn? It is Christ [Jesus] who died, rather, was raised, who also is at the right hand of God, who indeed intercedes for us. What will separate us from the love of Christ? Will anguish, or distress, or persecution, or famine, or nakedness, or peril, or the sword? As it is written:
"For your sake we are being slain all the day;
    we are looked upon as sheep to be slaughtered."
No, in all these things we conquer overwhelmingly through him who loved us. For I am convinced that neither death, nor life, nor angels, nor principalities, nor present things, nor future things, nor powers, nor height, nor depth, nor any other creature will be able to separate us from the love of God in Christ Jesus our Lord. ROMANS 8:31–39

"Peace I leave with you; my peace I give to you. Not as the world gives do I give it to you. Do not let your hearts be troubles or afraid." JOHN 14:27

"Amen, amen, I say to you, you will weep and mourn, while the world rejoices; you will grieve, but your grief will become joy. When a woman is in labour, she is in anguish because her hour has arrived; but when she has given birth to a child, she no longer remembers the pain because of her joy that a child has been born into the world. So you also are now in anguish. But I will see you again, and your hearts will rejoice, and no one will take your joy away from you."

JOHN 16:20–22

"Do not let your hearts be troubled. You have faith in God; have faith also in me." JOHN 14:1

You who fear the LORD, wait for his mercy,
    turn not away lest you fall.
You who fear the LORD, trust him,
    and your reward will not be lost.
You who fear the LORD, hope for good things,
    for lasting joy and mercy.
Study the generations long past and understand;
    has anyone hoped in the LORD and been
      disappointed?
Has anyone persevered in his fear and been forsaken?
    has anyone called upon him and been rebuffed?
Compassionate and merciful is the LORD;
    he forgives sins, he saves in time of trouble.
                           SIRACH 2:7–11

Let us fall into the hands of the LORD
    and not into the hands of men,
For equal to his majesty
    is the mercy that he shows. SIRACH 2:18

For every way, O LORD! you magnified and glorified
    your people;
    unfailing, you stood by them in every time and
    circumstance. WISDOM 19:22

Blessed day by day be the LORD,
    who bears our burdens; God, who is our salvation.
God is a saving God for us;
    the LORD, my Lord, controls the passageways of
    death. PSALM 68:20–21

God indeed will not delay,
    and like a warrior, will not be still
Till he breaks the backs of the merciless
    and wreaks vengeance upon the proud;
Till he destroys the haughty root and branch,
    and smashes the sceptre of the wicked;
Till he requires mankind according to its deeds,
    and repays men according to their thoughts;
Till he defends the cause of his people,
    and gladdens them by his mercy.
Welcome is his mercy in time of distress
    as rain clouds in time of drought.
               SIRACH 35:19–24

Now who is going to harm you if you are enthusiastic for what is good? But even if you should suffer because of righteousness, blessed are you. Do not be afraid or terrified with fear of them, but sanctify Christ as Lord in your hearts. 1 PETER 3:13–15a

13

When Feeling Lonely, Deserted or Unloved

Do not give in to sadness,
  torment not yourself with brooding;
Gladness of heart is the very life of man,
  cheerfulness prolongs his days.
Distract yourself, renew your courage,
  drive resentment far away from you;
For worry has brought death to many,
  nor is there aught to be gained from resentment.
Envy and anger shorten one's life,
  worry brings on premature old age.
One who is cheerful and gay while at table
  benefits from his food. SIRACH 30:21–25

For you are my hope, O Lord;
  my trust, O God, from my youth. PSALM 71:5

It crushes my bones that my foes mock me,
  as they say to me day after day, "Where is your
    God?" PSALM 42:11

Love the LORD, all you his faithful ones!
  the LORD keeps those who are constant,
  but more than requites those who act proudly.
                                        PSALM 31:24

For in him our hearts rejoice;
  in his holy name we trust. PSALM 33:21

Yet will I rejoice in the LORD
  and exult in my saving God. HABAKKUK 3:18

. . . so that by two immutable things, in which it was impossible for God to lie, we who have taken refuge might be strongly encouraged to hold fast to the hope that lies before us. This we have as an anchor of the soul, sure and firm, which reaches into the interior behind the veil, . . . HEBREWS 6:18–19

On this account I am suffering these things; but I am not ashamed, for I know him in whom I have believed and am confident that he is able to guard what has been entrusted to me until that day. 2 TIMOTHY 1:12

Thus says the LORD: In this place of which you say, "How desolate it is, without man, without beast!" and in the cities of Judah, in the streets of Jerusalem that are not deserted, without man, without citizen, without beast, there shall yet be heard the cry of joy, the cry of gladness, the voice of the bridegroom, the voice of the bride, the sound of those who bring thank offerings to the house of the LORD, singing, "Give thanks to the LORD of hosts, for the LORD is good; his mercy endures forever." For I will restore this country as of old, says the LORD. JEREMIAH 33:10–11

He heals the brokenhearted
  and binds up their wounds. PSALM 147:3

Yes, in joy you shall depart,
   in peace you shall be brought back;
Mountains and hills shall break out in song before
    you,
   and all the trees of the countryside shall clap their
    hands. ISAIAH 55:12

"Do not let your hearts be troubled. You have faith in God; have faith also in me. In my Father's house there are many dwelling places. If there were not, would I have told you that I am going to prepare a place for you? And if I go and prepare a place for you, I will come back again and take you to myself, so that where I am you also may be. Where [I] am going you know the way." JOHN 14:1–4

"As the Father loves me, so I also love you. Remain in my love. If you keep my commandments, you will remain in my love, just as I have kept my Father's commandments and remain in his love.

"I have told you this so that my joy might be in you and your joy might be complete." JOHN 15:9–11

"Amen, amen, I say to you, you will weep and mourn, while the world rejoices; you will grieve, but your grief will become joy. When a woman is in labour, she is in anguish because her hour has arrived, but when she has given birth to a child, she no longer remembers the pain because of her joy that a child has been born into the world. So you also are now in anguish. But I will see you again, and your hearts will rejoice, and no one will take your joy away from you. On that day you will not question me about anything. Amen, amen, I say to you, whatever you ask the Father in my name he will give you." JOHN 16:20–23

"Until now you have not asked anything in my name; ask and you will receive, so that your joy may be complete . . . For the Father himself loves you, because you have loved me and have come to believe that I came from God." JOHN 16:24, 27.

Therefore, since we have been justified by faith, we have peace with God through our Lord Jesus Christ, through whom we have gained access [by faith] to this grace in which we stand, and we boast in hope of the glory of God. Not only that, but we even boast of our afflictions, knowing that affliction produces endurance, and endurance, proven character, and proven character, hope, and hope does not disappoint, because the love of God has been poured out into our hearts through the holy Spirit that has been given to us. ROMANS 5:1–5

We know that all things work for good for those who love God, who are called according to his purpose. For those he foreknew he also predestined to be conformed to the image of his Son, so that he might be the firstborn among many brothers. And those he predestined he also called; and those he called he also justified; and those he justified he also glorified.

When then shall we say to this? If God is for us, who can be against us? He who did not spare his own Son but handed him over for us all, how will he not also give us everything else along with him? Who will condemn? It is Christ [Jesus] who died, rather, was raised, who also is at the right hand of God, who indeed intercedes for us. ROMANS 8:28–34

What will separate us from the love of Christ? Will anguish, or distress, or persecution, or famine, or nakedness, or peril, or the sword? As it is written: "For your sake we are being slain all the day;
   we are looked upon as sheep to be slaughtered."
No, in all these things we conquer overwhelmingly through him who loved us. For I am convinced that neither death, nor life, nor angels, nor principalities, nor present things, nor future things, nor powers, nor height, nor depth, nor any other creature will be able to separate us from the love of God in Christ Jesus our Lord. ROMANS 8:35–39

Rejoice in the Lord always. I shall say it again: rejoice! Your kindness should be known to all. The Lord is near. Have no anxiety at all, but in everything, by prayer and petition, with thanksgiving, make your requests known to God. Then the peace of God that surpasses all understanding will guard your hearts and minds in Christ Jesus. PHILIPPIANS 4:4–7

Finally, brothers, whatever is true, whatever is honourable, whatever is just, whatever is pure, whatever is lovely, whatever is gracious, if there is any excellence and if there is anything worthy of praise, think about these things. Keep on doing what you have learned and received and heard and seen in me. Then the God of peace will be with you.

PHILIPPIANS 4:8–9

Put on then, as God's chosen ones, holy and beloved, heartfelt compassion, kindness, humility, gentleness, and patience, bearing with one another and forgiving one another, if one has a grievance against another; as the Lord has forgiven you, so must you also do. And over all these put on love, that is, the bond of perfection. And let the peace of Christ control your hearts, the peace into which you were also called in one body. And be thankful.

COLOSSIANS 3:12–15

IV

God and Our Personal Relationships

14

Parents

Train a boy in the way he should go;
    even when he is old, he will not swerve from it.
                                PROVERBS 22:6

Your wife shall be like a fruitful vine
    in the recesses of your home;
Your children like olive plants
    around your table.
Behold, thus is the man blessed
    who fears the LORD.
The LORD bless you from Zion:
    may you see the prosperity of Jerusalem
    all the days of your life;
May you see your children's children.
    Peace be upon Israel! PSALM 128:3–6

May the LORD bless you more and more,
    both you and your children. PSALM 115:14

Behold, sons are a gift from the LORD;
    the fruit of the womb is a reward.
Like arrows in the hand of a warrior
    are the sons of one's youth.
Happy the man whose quiver is filled with them;
    they shall not be put to shame when they contend
    with enemies at the gate. PSALM 127:3–5

Lo, I will send you
  Elijah, the prophet,
Before the day of the LORD comes,
  the great and terrible day,
To turn the hearts of the fathers to their children,
  and the hearts of the children to their fathers,
Lest I come and strike
  the land with doom. MALACHI 3:23–24

"Honour your father and your mother, that you may
have a long life in the land which the Lord, your God,
is giving you." EXODUS 20:12

The good man leaves an inheritance to his children's
      children,
    but the wealth of the sinner is stored up for the
      just. PROVERBS 13:22

He who spares his rod hates his son,
  but he who loves him takes care to chastise him.
                              PROVERBS 13:24

Grandchildren are the crown of old men,
  and the glory of children is their parentage.
                          PROVERBS 17:6

Chastise your son, for in this there is hope;
  but do not desire his death. PROVERBS 19:18

He who mistreats his father, or drives away his
      mother,
    is a worthless and disgraceful son. PROVERBS 19:26

Parents

If one curses his father or mother,
  his lamp will go out at the coming of darkness.
                                            PROVERBS 20:20

Correct your son, and he will bring you comfort,
  and give delight to your soul. PROVERBS 29:17

He who loves his son chastises him often,
  that he may be his joy when he grows up.
He who disciplines his son will benefit from him,
  and boast of him among his intimates.
He who educates his son makes his enemy jealous,
  and shows his delight in him among his friends.
                                            SIRACH 30:1–3

Pamper your child and he will be a terror for you,
  indulge him and he will bring you grief.
Share not in his frivolity lest you share in his sorrow,
  when finally your teeth are clenched in remorse.
Give him not his own way in his youth,
  and close not your eyes to his follies.
Bend him to the yoke when he is young,
  thrash his sides while he is still small,
Lest he become stubborn, disobey you,
  and leave you disconsolate.
Discipline your son, make heavy his yoke,
  lest his folly humiliate you. SIRACH 30:9–13

Fathers, do not provoke your children, so they may
not become discouraged. COLOSSIANS 3:21

Fathers, do not provoke your children to anger, but
bring them up with the training and instruction of the
Lord. EPHESIANS 6:4

And whoever does not provide for relatives and especially family members has denied the faith and is worse than an unbeliever. 1 TIMOTHY 5:8

Can a mother forget her infant,
    be without tenderness for the child of her womb?
Even should she forget,
    I will never forget you.
See, upon the palms of my hands I have written your
      name;
    Your walls are ever before me. ISAIAH 49:15–16

This is the covenant with them
    which I myself have made, says the LORD:
My spirit which is upon you
    and my words that I have put into your mouth
Shall never leave your mouth,
    nor the mouths of your children
Nor the mouths of your childen's children
    from now on and forever, says the LORD.
                    ISAIAH 59:21

15

Children

"Honour your father and your mother, that you may have a long life in the land which the Lord, your God, is giving you." EXODUS 20:12

Hear, my son, your father's instruction,
    and reject not your mother's teaching;
A graceful diadem will they be for your head;
    a torque for your neck. PROVERBS 1:8–9

My son, let not these slip out of your sight:
    keep advice and counsel in view;
So will they be life to your soul,
    and an adornment for your neck.
Then you may securely go your way;
    your foot will never stumble;
When you lie down, you need not be afraid,
    when you rest, your sleep will be sweet.
                        PROVERBS 3:21–24

The path of the wicked enter not,
    walk not on the way of evil men; . . .
                        PROVERBS 4:14

Honour your father and your mother, as the LORD, your God, has commanded you, that you may have a long life and prosperity in the land which the LORD, your God, is giving you. DEUTERONOMY 5:16

Hear, my son, and receive my words,
    and the years of your life shall be many.
On the way of wisdom I direct you,
    I lead you on straightforward paths.
                PROVERBS 4:10–11

My son, to my words be attentive,
    to my sayings incline your ear;
Let them not slip out of your sight,
    keep them within your heart;
For they are life to those who find them,
    to man's whole being they are health.
                PROVERBS 4:20–22

Observe, my son, your father's bidding,
    and reject not your mother's teaching;
Keep them fastened over your heart always,
    put them around your neck;
For the bidding is a lamp, and the teaching a light,
    and a way to life are the reproofs of discipline;
To keep you from your neighbour's wife,
    from the smooth tongue of the adulteress.
                PROVERBS 6:20–24

A son who fills the granaries in summer is a credit;
    A son who slumbers during harvest, a disgrace.
                PROVERBS 10:5

The rod of correction gives wisdom,
    but a boy left to his whims disgraces his mother.
                PROVERBS 29:15

Children

A wise son loves correction,
    but the senseless one heeds no rebuke.
PROVERBS 13:1

Hear, my son, and be wise,
    and guide your heart in the right way.
Consort not with winebibbers,
    nor with those who eat meat to excess;
For the drunkard and the glutton come to poverty,
    and torpor clothes a man in rags.
Listen to your father who begot you,
    and despise not your mother when she is old.
Get the truth, and sell it not —
    wisdom, instruction and understanding.
PROVERBS 23:19–23

Children, pay heed to a father's right;
    do so that you may live
for the LORD sets a father in honour over his children;
    a mother's authority he confirms over her sons.
He who honours his father atones for sins;
    he stores up riches who reveres his mother.
He who honours his father is gladdened by children,
    and when he prays he is heard.
He who reveres his father will live a long life;
    he obeys the LORD who brings comfort to his
        mother.
He who fears the LORD honours his father,
    and serves his parents as rulers. SIRACH 3:1–7

My son, take care of your father when he is old;
    grieve him not as long as he lives.
Even if his mind fail, be considerate with him;

revile him not in the fullness of your strength.
For kindness to a father will not be forgotten,
   it will serve as a sin offering – it will take lasting
      root.
In time of tribulation it will be recalled to your
      advantage,
   like warmth upon frost it will melt away your sins.
A blasphemer is he who despises his father;
   accursed of his Creator, he who angers his mother.
                                        SIRACH 3:12–16

My son, from your youth embrace discipline;
   thus will you find wisdom with greying hair.
As though ploughing and sowing, draw close to her;
   then await her bountiful crops. SIRACH 6:18–19

My son, if you wish, you can be taught;
   if you apply yourself, you will be shrewd.
If you are willing to listen, you will learn;
   if you give heed, you will be wise.
Frequent the company of the elders;
   whoever is wise, stay close to him.
Be eager to hear every godly discourse;
   let no wise saying escape you.
If you see a man of prudence, seek him out;
   let your feet wear away his doorstep!
Reflect on the precepts of the LORD,
   let his commandments be your constant
      meditation;
Then he will enlighten your mind,
   and the wisdom you desire he will grant.
                                        SIRACH 6:32–37

Whose offspring can be in honour? Those of men.
  Which offspring are in honour? Those who fear
    God.
Whose offspring can be in disgrace? Those of men.
  Which offspring are in disgrace?
  Those who transgress the commandments.

SIRACH 10:19

My son, hold fast to your duty, busy yourself with it,
  grow old while doing your task.
Admire not how sinners live,
  but trust in the LORD and wait for his light;
For it is easy with the LORD
  suddenly, in an instant, to make a poor man rich.
God's blessing is the lot of the just man,
  and in due time his hopes bear fruit.
Say not: "What do I need?
  What further pleasure can be mine?"
Say not: "I am independent.
  What harm can come to me now?"
The day of prosperity makes one forget adversity;
  the day of adversity makes one forget prosperity.
For it is easy with the LORD on the day of death
  to repay man according to his deeds.

SIRACH 11:20–26

Children, obey your parents in everything, for this is
pleasing to the Lord. COLOSSIANS 3:20

Children, obey your parents [in the Lord], for this
is right. "Honour your father and mother." This is the
first commandment with a promise, "that it may go

well with you and that you may have a long life on earth." EPHESIANS 6:1–3

. . . but Jesus said, "Let the children come to me, and do not prevent them; for the kingdom of heaven belongs to such as these." MATTHEW 19:14

My son, if you have sinned, do so no more,
    and for your past sins pray to be forgiven.
Flee from sin as from a serpent
    that will bite you if you go near it;
Its teeth are lion's teeth,
    destroying the souls of men.
Every offence is a two-edged sword;
    when it cuts, there can be no healing.
Violence and arrogance wipe out wealth;
    so too a proud man's home is destroyed.
                    SIRACH 21:1–4

Let not your mouth become used to coarse talk,
    for in it lies sinful matter.
Keep your father and mother in mind
    when you sit among the mighty,
Lest in their presence you commit a blunder
    and disgrace your upbringing,
By wishing you had never been born
    or cursing the day of your birth.
A man who has the habit of abusive language
    will never mature in character as long as he lives.
                    SIRACH 23:13–15

Children

A wise son makes his father glad,
  but a fool of a man despises his mother.
                              PROVERBS 15:20

Though my father and mother forsake me,
  yet will the LORD receive me. PSALM 27:10

16

Husbands and Wives

"For this reason a man shall leave [his] father and
    [his] mother
    and be joined to his wife,
and the two shall become one flesh."
This is a great mystery, but I speak in reference to
Christ and the church. In any case, each one of you
should love his wife as himself, and the wife should
respect her husband. EPHESIANS 5:31–33

A gracious wife delights her husband,
    her thoughtfulness puts flesh on his bones;
A gift from the LORD is her governed speech,
    and her firm virtue is surpassing worth.
Choicest of blessings is a modest wife,
    priceless her chaste person.
Like the sun rising in the LORD's heavens,
    the beauty of a virtuous wife is the radiance of her
        home.
Like the light which shines above the holy
        lampstand,
    are her beauty of face and graceful figure.
Golden columns on silver bases
    are her shapely limbs and steady feet.
                        SIRACH 26:13–18

A woman's beauty makes her husband's face light up,
    for it surpasses all else that charms the eye;

And if, besides, her speech is kindly,
    his lot is beyond that of mortal men.
A wife is her husband's richest treasure,
    a helpmate, a steadying column. SIRACH 36:22–24

When one finds a worthy wife,
    her value is far beyond pearls.
Her husband, entrusting his heart to her,
    has an unfailing prize.
She brings him good, and not evil,
    all the days of her life.
She obtains wool and flax
    and makes cloth with skillful hands.
Like merchant ships,
    she secures her provisions from afar.
She rises while it is still night,
    and distributes food to her household.
She picks out a field to purchase;
    out of her earnings she plants a vineyard.
She is girt about with strength,
    and sturdy are her arms.
She enjoys the success of her dealings;
    at night her lamp is undimmed.
She puts her hands to the distaff,
    and her fingers ply the spindle.
She reaches out her hands to the poor,
    and extends her arms to the needy.
She fears not the snow for her household;
    all her charges are doubly clothed.
She makes her own coverlets;
    fine linen and purple are her clothing.
Her husband is prominent at the city gates
    as he sits with the elders of the land.

She makes garments and sells them,
    and stocks the merchants with belts.
She is clothed with strength and dignity,
    and she laughs at the days to come.
She opens her mouth in wisdom,
    and on her tongue is kindly counsel.
She watches the conduct of her household,
    and eats not her food in idleness.
Her children rise up and praise her;
    her husband, too extols her:
"Many are the women of proven worth,
    but you have excelled them all."
Charm is deceptive and beauty fleeting;
    the woman who fears the LORD is to be praised.
Give her a reward of her labours,
    and let her works praise her at the city gates.

                   PROVERBS 31:10–31

Drink water from your own cistern,
    running water from your own well.
How may your water sources be dispersed abroad,
    streams of water in the streets?
Let your fountain be yours alone,
    not one shared with strangers;
And have the joy of the wife of your youth,
    your lovely hind, your graceful doe.
Her love will invogorate you always,
    through her love you will flourish continually,
When you lie down she will watch over you,
    and when you wake, she will share your concerns;
    wherever you turn, she will guide you.

                   PROVERBS 5:15–19

Husbands and Wives

But he who commits adultery is a fool;
　　he who would destroy himself does it.
A degrading beating will he get,
　　and his disgrace will not be wiped away; . . .
PROVERBS 6:32–33

Home and possessions are an inheritance from
　　　parents,
　　but a prudent wife is from the LORD.
PROVERBS 19:14

Be not jealous of the wife of your bosom,
　　lest you teach her to do evil against you.
SIRACH 9:1

With three things I am delighted,
　　for they are pleasing to the LORD, and to men:
Harmony among brethren, friendship among
　　　neighbours,
　　and the mutual love of husband and wife.
SIRACH 25:1

A jealous wife is heartache and mourning
　　and a scourging tongue like the other three.
A bad wife is a chafing yoke;
　　he who marries her seizes a scorpion.
A drunken wife arouses great anger,
　　for she does not hide her shame.
By her eyelids and her haughty stare
　　an unchaste wife can be recognized.
SIRACH 26:6–9

The LORD God said: "It is not good for the man to be alone. I will make a suitable partner for him." . . .

That is why a man leaves his father and mother and clings to his wife, and the two of them become one body. GENESIS 2:18, 24

Some Pharisees approached him, and tested him, saying, "Is it lawful for a man to divorce his wife for any cause whatever?" He said in reply, "Have you not read that from the beginning the Creator 'made them male and female' and said, 'For this reason a man shall leave his father and mother and be joined to his wife, and the two shall become one flesh'? So they are no longer two, but one flesh. Therefore, what God has joined together, no human being must separate."

MATTHEW 19:3–6

Happy are you who fear the LORD,
    who walk in his ways!
For you shall eat the fruit of your handiwork;
    happy shall you be, and favoured.
Your wife shall be like a fruitful vine
    in the recesses of your home;
Your children like olive plants
    around your table.
Behold, thus is the man blessed
    who fears the LORD.
The LORD bless you from Zion:
    may you see the prosperity of Jerusalem
    all the days of your life;
May you see your children's children.
    Peace be upon Israel! PSALM 128:1–6

"It was also said, 'Whoever divorces his wife must give her a bill of divorce.' But I say to you, whoever divorces his wife (unless the marriage is unlawful) causes her to commit adultery, and whoever marries a divorced woman commits adultery."

MATTHEW 5:31–32

Likewise, you wives should be subordinate to your husbands so that, even if some disobey the word, they may be won over without a word by their wives' conduct when they observe your reverent and chaste behaviour. Your adornment should not be an external one: braiding the hair, wearing gold jewellery, or dressing in fine clothes, but rather the hidden character of the heart, expressed in the imperishable beauty of a gentle and calm disposition, which is precious in the sight of God. For this is also how the holy women who hoped in God once used to adorn themselves and were subordinate to their husbands; thus Sarah obeyed Abraham, calling him "lord". You are her children when you do what is good and fear no intimidation. 1 PETER 3:1–6

The husband should fulfill his duty toward his wife, and likewise the wife toward her husband. A wife does not have authority over her own body, but rather her husband, and similarly a husband does not have authority over his own body, but rather his wife. Do not deprive each other, except perhaps by mutual consent for a time, to be free for prayer, but then return to one another, so that Satan may not tempt you through your lack of self-control.

1 CORINTHIANS 7:3–5

Enjoy life with the wife whom you love, all the days of the fleeting life that is granted you under the sun. This is your lot in life, for the toil of your labours under the sun. ECCLESIASTES 9:9

Likewise, you husbands should live with your wives in understanding, showing honour to the weaker female sex, since we are joint heirs of the gift of life, so that your prayers may not be hindered. 1 PETER 3:7

A wife is bound to her husband as long as he lives. But if her husband dies, she is free to be married to whomever she wishes, provided that it be in the Lord.
1 CORINTHIANS 7:39

And you say, "Why is it?" –
   Because the LORD is witness
   between you and the wife of your youth,
With whom you have broken faith
   though she is your companion, your betrothed
     wife.
Did he not make one being, with flesh and spirit:
   and what does that one require but godly
     offspring?
You must then safeguard life that is your own,
   and not break faith with the wife of your youth.
For I hate divorce,
   says the LORD the God of Israel,
And covering one's garment with injustice,
   says the LORD of hosts;
You must then safeguard life that is your own,
   and not break faith. MALACHI 2:14–16

17

Brothers and Sisters in the Body of Christ

Behold, how good it is, and how pleasant,
  where brethren dwell at one!
It is as when the precious ointment upon the head
  runs down over the beard, the beard of Aaron,
  till it runs down upon the collar of his robe.
It is a dew like that of Hermon,
  which comes down upon the mountains of Zion;
For there the LORD has pronounced his blessing,
  life forever. PSALM 133:1b–3

"But I say to you, love your enemies, and pray for those who persecute you, that you may be children of your heavenly Father, for he makes his sun rise on the bad and the good, and causes rain to fall on the just and the unjust. For if you love those who love you, what recompense will you have? Do not the tax collectors do the same? And if you greet your brothers only, what is unusual about that? Do not the pagans do the same? So be perfect, just as your heavenly Father is perfect." MATTHEW 5:44–48

While he was still speaking to the crowds, his mother and his brothers appeared outside, wishing to speak with him. [Someone told him, "Your mother and your brothers are standing outside, asking to speak with you."] But he said in reply to the one who told him, "Who is my mother? Who are my brothers?" And stretching out his hand toward his disciples, he said, "Here are my mother and my brothers. For whoever does the will of my heavenly Father is my brother, and sister, and mother." MATTHEW 12:46–50

"If you forgive others their transgressions, your heavenly Father will forgive you. But if you do not forgive others, neither will your Father forgive your transgressions." MATTHEW 6:14–15

"See that you do not despise one of these little ones, for I say to you that their angels in heaven always look upon the face of my heavenly Father. What is your opinion? If a man has a hundred sheep and one of them goes astray, will he not leave the ninety-nine in the hills and go in search of the stray? And if he finds it, amen, I say to you, he rejoices more over it than over the ninety-nine that did not stray. In just the same way, it is not the will of your heavenly Father that one of these little ones be lost.'

MATTHEW 18:10–14

"Again, [amen,] I say to you, if two of you agree on earth about anything for which they are to pray, it shall be granted to them by my heavenly Father. For where two or three are gathered together in my name, there am I in the midst of them." MATTHEW 18:19–20

They came to Capernaum and, once inside the house, he began to ask them, "What were you arguing about on the way?" But they remained silent. They had been discussing among themselves on the way who was the greatest. Then he sat down, called the

Twelve, and said to them, "If anyone wishes to be first, he shall be the last of all and the servant of all."

MARK 9:33–35

Then an argument broke out among them about which of them should be regarded as the greatest. He said to them, "The kings of the Gentiles lord it over them and those in authority over them are addressed as 'Benefactors'; but among you it shall not be so. Rather, let the greatest among you be as the youngest, and the leader as the servant. For who is greater: the one seated at table or the one who serves? Is it not the one seated at table? I am among you as the one who serves. It is you who have stood by me in my trials; and I confer a kingdom on you, just as my Father has conferred one on me, that you may eat and drink at my table in my kingdom; and you will sit on thrones judging the twelve tribes of Israel." LUKE 22:24–30

So when he had washed their feet [and] put his garments back on and reclined at table again, he said to them, "Do you realize what I have done for you? You call me 'teacher' and 'master', and rightly so, for indeed I am. If I, therefore, the master and teacher, have washed your feet, you ought to wash one another's feet. I have given you a model to follow, so that as I have done for you, you should also do. Amen, amen, I say to you, no slave is greater than his master nor any messenger greater than the one who sent him. If you understand this, blessed are you if you do it."

JOHN 13:12–17

"I give you a new commandment: love one another. As I have loved you, so you also should love one another. This is how all will know that you are my disciples, if you have love for one another."

JOHN 13:34–35

"This is my commandment: love one another as I love you. No one has greater love than this, to lay down one's life for one's friends. You are my friends if you do what I command you . . . This I command you: love one another." JOHN 15:12–14, 17

"I pray not only for them, but also for those who will believe in me through their word, so that they may all be one, as you, Father, are in me and I in you, that they also may be in us, that the world may believe that you sent me. And I have given them the glory you gave me, so that they may be one, as we are one, I in them and you in me, that they may be brought to perfection as one, that the world may know that you sent me, and that you loved them even as you loved me." JOHN 17:20–23

Beloved, do not look for revenge but leave room for the wrath; for it is written, "Vengeance is mine, I will repay, says the Lord." Rather, "if your enemy is hungry, feed him; if he is thirsty, give him something to drink; for by so doing you will heap burning coals upon his head." Do not be conquered by evil but conquer evil with good. ROMANS 12:19–21

Owe nothing to anyone, except to love one another; for the one who loves another has fulfilled the law.

The commandments, "You shall not commit adultery; you shall not kill, you shall not steal; you shall not covet," and whatever other commandment there may be, are summed up in this saying,[namely] "You shall love your neighbours as yourself." Love does no evil to the neighbour; hence, love is the fulfilment of the law.

ROMANS 13:8–10

None of us lives for oneself, and no one dies for oneself. For if we live, we live for the Lord, and if we die, we die for the Lord; so then, whether we live or die, we are the Lord's. For this is why Christ died and came to life, that he might be Lord of both the dead and the living. Why then do you judge your brother? Or you, why do you look down on your brother? For we shall all stand before the judgement seat of God; for it is written:
"As I live, says the Lord, every knee shall bend before me,

and every tongue shall give praise to God."

ROMANS 14:7–11

So [then] each of us shall give an account of himself [to God].

Then let us no longer judge one another, but rather resolve never to put a stumbling block or hindrance in the way of a brother . . . Let us then pursue what leads to peace and to building up one another.

ROMANS 14:12–13, 19

We who are strong ought to put up with the failings of the weak and not to please ourselves; let each of us please our neighbour for the good, for building up.

For Christ did not please himself; but, as it is written, "The insults of those who insult you fall upon me." For whatever was written previously was written for our instruction, that by endurance and by the encouragement of the scriptures we might have hope. May the God of endurance and encouragement grant you to think in harmony with one another, in keeping with Christ Jesus, that with one accord you may with one voice glorify the God and Father of our Lord Jesus Christ. ROMANS 15:1–6

Consider your own calling, brothers. Not many of you were wise by human standards, not many were powerful, not many were of noble birth. Rather, God chose the foolish of the world to shame the wise, and God chose the weak of the world to shame the strong, and God chose the lowly and despised of the world, those who count for nothing, to reduce to nothing those who are something, so that no human being might boast before God. It is due to him that you are in Christ Jesus, who became for us wisdom from God, as well as righteousness, sanctification, and redemption, so that, as it is written, "Whoever boasts, should boast in the Lord." CORINTHIANS 1:26–31

Therefore, neither the one who plants nor the one who waters is anything, but only God, who causes the growth. The one who plants and the one who waters are equal, and each will receive wages in proportion to his labour. For we are God's co-workers; you are God's field, God's building. 1 CORINTHIANS 3:7–9

There are different kinds of spiritual gifts but the same Spirit; there are different forms of service but the same Lord; there are different workings but the same God who produces all of them in everyone. To each individual the manifestation of the Spirit is given for some benefit. To one is given through the Spirit the expression of wisdom; to another the expression of knowledge according to the same Spirit; to another faith by the same Spirit; to another gifts of healing by the one Spirit; to another mighty deeds; to another prophecy; to another discernment of spirits; to another varieties of tongues; to another interpretation of tongues. But one and the same Spirit produces all of these, distributing them individually to each person as he wishes.
1 CORINTHIANS 12:4–11

If I speak in human and angelic tongues but do not have love, I am a resounding gong or a clashing cymbal. And if I have the gift of prophecy and comprehend all mysteries and all knowledge; if I have all faith so as to move mountains, but do not have love, I am nothing. If I give away everything I own, and if I hand my body over so that I may boast but do not have love, I gain nothing.

Love is patient, love is kind. It is not jealous, [love] is not pompous, it is not inflated, it is not rude, it does not seek its own interests, it is not quick-tempered, it does not brood over injury, it does not rejoice over wrongdoing but rejoices with the truth. It bears all things, believes all things, hopes all things, endures all things.

Love never fails. If there are prophecies, they will be brought to nothing; if tongues, they will cease; if

141

knowledge, it will be brought to nothing. For we know partially and we prophesy partially, but when the perfect comes, the partial will pass away. When I was a child, I used to talk as a child, think as a child, reason as a child; when I became a man, I put aside childish things. At present we see indistinctly, as in a mirror, but then face to face. At present I know partially; then I shall know fully, as I am fully known. So faith, hope, love remain, these three; but the greatest of these is love. 1 CORINTHIANS 13

Consider this; whoever sows sparingly will also reap sparingly, and whoever sows bountifully will also reap bountifully. Each must do as already determined, without sadness or compulsion, for God loves a cheerful giver. Moreover, God is able to make every grace abundant for you, so that in all things, always having all you need, you may have an abundance for every good work. As it is written:
"He scatters abroad, he gives to the poor;
    his righteousness endures forever."
The one who supplies seed to the sower and bread for food will supply and multiply your seed and increase the harvest of your righteousness.

You are being enriched in every way for all generosity, which through us produces thanksgiving to God, for the administration of this public service is not only supplying the needs of the holy ones but is also overflowing in many acts of thanksgiving to God. Through the evidence of this service, you are glorifying God for your obedient confession of the gospel of Christ and the generosity of your contribution to them and to all others, . . . 2 CORINTHIANS 9:6–13

Finally, all of you, be of one mind, sympathetic, loving toward one another, compassionate, humble. Do not return evil for evil, or insult for insult; but, on the contrary, a blessing, because of this you were called, that you might inherit a blessing.

1 PETER 3:8–9

Rejoice in the Lord always. I shall say it again: rejoice! Your kindness should be known to all. The Lord is near. Have no anxiety at all, but in everything, by prayer and petition, with thanksgiving, make your requests known to God. Then the peace of God that surpasses all understanding will guard your hearts and minds in Christ Jesus. PHILIPPIANS 4:4–7

Finally, brothers, whatever is true, whatever is honourable, whatever is just, whatever is pure, whatever is lovely, whatever is gracious, if there is any excellence and if there is anything worthy of praise, think about these things. Keep on doing what you have learned and received and heard and seen in me. Then the God of peace will be with you.

PHILIPPIANS 4:8–9

Put to death, then, the parts of you that are earthly: immorality, impurity, passion, evil desire, and the greed that is idolatry. Because of these the wrath of God is coming [upon the disobedient]. By these you too once conducted yourselves, when you lived in that way. But now you must put them all away; anger, fury, malice, slander, and obscene language out of your mouths. Stop lying to one another, since you have taken off the old self with its practices and have put on the new self, which is being renewed, for knowledge, in the image of its creator.

COLOSSIANS 3:5–10

Finally, brothers, rejoice. Mend your ways, encourage one another, agree with one another, live in peace, and the God of love and peace will be with you . . .

The grace of the Lord Jesus Christ and the love of God and the fellowship of the holy Spirit be with all of you. 2 CORINTHIANS 13:11, 13

Beloved, if God so loved us, we also must love one another. No one has ever seen God. Yet, if we love one another, God remains in us, and his love is brought to perfection in us. 1 JOHN 4:11–12

For God is not unjust so as to overlook your work and the love you have demonstrated for his name by having served and continuing to serve the holy ones.

HEBREWS 6:10

V

God's Promises to the Church

18

Unity

"I pray not only for them, but also those who will believe in me through their word, so that they may all be one, as you, Father, are in me and I in you, that they also may be in us, that the world may believe that you sent me. And I have given them the glory you gave me, so that they may be one, as we are one, I in them and you in me, that they may be brought to perfection as one, that the world may know that you sent me, and that you loved them even as you loved me." JOHN 17:20–23

So then you are no longer strangers and sojourners, but you are fellow citizens with the holy ones and members of the household of God, built upon the foundation of the apostles and prophets, with Christ Jesus himself as the capstone. Through him the whole structure is held together and grows into a temple sacred in the Lord; in him you also are being built together into a dwelling place of God in the Spirit.

EPHESIANS 2:19–22

And he gave some as apostles, others as prophets, others as evangelists, others as pastors and teachers, to equip the holy ones for the work of ministry, for building up the body of Christ, until we all attain to the unity of faith and knowledge of the Son of God, to mature manhood, to the extent of the full stature of Christ, so that we may no longer be infants, tossed by waves and swept along by every wind of teaching arising from human trickery, from their cunning in the interests of deceitful scheming. Rather, living the truth in love, we should grow in every way into him who is the head, Christ, from whom the whole body, joined and held together by every supporting ligament, with the proper functioning of each part, brings about the body's growth and builds itself up in love.

EPHESIANS 4:11–16

The cup of blessing that we bless, is it not a participation in the blood of Christ? The bread that we break, is it not a participation in the body of Christ? Because the loaf of bread is one, we, though many, are one body, for we all partake of the one loaf.

1 CORINTHIANS 10:16–17

As a body is one though it has many parts, and all the parts of the body, though many, are one body, so also Christ. For in one Spirit we were all baptized into one body, whether Jews or Greeks, slaves or free persons, and we were all given to drink of one Spirit.

1 CORINTHIANS 12:12–13

But now in Christ Jesus you who were far off have become near by the blood of Christ.

For he is our peace, he who made both one and broke down the dividing wall of enmity, through his flesh, abolishing the law with its commandments and legal claims, that he might create in himself one new person in place of the two, thus establishing peace, and might reconcile both with God, in one body, through the cross, putting that enmity to death by it. He came and preached peace to you who were far off and peace to those who were near, . . .

EPHESIANS 2:13–17

I, then, a prisoner for the Lord, urge you to live in a manner worthy of the call you have received, with all humility and gentleness, with patience, bearing with one another through love, striving to preserve the unity of the spirit through the bond of peace; one body and one Spirit, as you were also called to the one hope of your call; one Lord, one faith, one baptism; one God and Father of all, who is over all and through all and in all. EPHESIANS 4:1–6

If there is any encouragement in Christ, any solace in love, any participation in the Spirit, any compassion and mercy, complete my joy by being of the same mind, with the same love, united in heart, thinking one thing. Do nothing out of selfishness or out of vainglory; rather, humbly regard others as more important than yourselves, each looking out not for his own interests, but [also] everyone for those of others. PHILIPPIANS 2:1–4

"I give you a new commandment: love one another. As I have loved you, so you also should love one another. This is how all will know that you are my disciples, if you have love for one another."

JOHN 13:34–35

19

Favours and Blessings

I will make you a light to the nations,
  that my salvation may reach to the ends of the
    earth.
Thus says the LORD,
  the redeemer and the Holy One of Israel,
To the one despised, whom the nations abhor,
  the slave of rulers;
When kings see you, they shall stand up,
  and princes shall prostrate themselves
Because of the LORD who is faithful,
  the Holy One of Israel who has chosen you.
                                 ISAIAH 49:6b–7

"My sheep hear my voice; I know them, and they follow me. I give them eternal life, and they shall never perish. No one can take them out of my hand. My Father, who has given them to me, is greater than all, and no one can take them out of the Father's hand." JOHN 10:27–29

Blessed be the God and Father of our Lord Jesus Christ, who in his great mercy gave us a new birth to a living hope through the resurrection of Jesus Christ from the dead, to an inheritance that is imperishable, undefiled, and unfading, kept in heaven for you who by the power of God are safeguarded through faith, to a salvation that is ready to be revealed in the final time. 1 PETER 1:3–5

Simon Peter said in reply, "You are the Messiah, the Son of the living God." Jesus said to him in reply, "Blessed are you, Simon son of Jonah. For flesh and blood has not revealed this to you, but my heavenly Father. And so I say to you, you are Peter, and upon this rock I will build my church, and the gates of the netherworld shall not prevail against it. I will give you the keys to the kingdom of heaven. Whatever you bind on earth shall be bound in heaven; and whatever you loose on earth shall be loosed in heaven."

MATTHEW 16:16–19

And Mary said:
"My soul proclaims the greatness of the Lord;
my spirit rejoices in God my saviour.
For he has looked upon his handmaid's lowliness;
    behold, from now on will all ages call me blessed.
The Mighty One has done great things for me,
    and holy is his name.
His mercy is from age to age
    to those who fear him." LUKE 1:46–50

When the time for Pentecost was fulfilled, they were all in one place together. ACTS 2:1

Come to him, a living stone, rejected by human beings but chosen and precious in the sight of God, and, like living stones, let yourselves be built into a spiritual

house to be a holy priesthood to offer spiritual sacrifices acceptable to God through Jesus Christ. For it says in scripture:
"Behold, I am laying a stone in Zion,
  a cornerstone, chosen and precious,
and whoever believes in it shall not be put to shame."
1 PETER 2:4–6

"You are my friends if you do what I command you. I no longer call you slaves, because a slave does not know what his master is doing. I have called you friends, because I have told you everything I have heard from my Father. It was not you who chose me, but I who chose you and appointed you to go and bear fruit that will remain, so that whatever you ask the Father in my name he may give you." JOHN 15:14–16

"But I tell you the truth, it is better for you that I go. For if I do not go, the Advocate will not come to you. But if I go, I will send him to you. And when he comes he will convict the world in regard to sin and righteousness and condemnation: sin, because they do not believe in me; righteousness, because I am going to the Father and you will no longer see me; condemnation, because the ruler of this world has been condemned.

"I have much more to tell you, but you cannot bear it now. But when he comes, the Spirit of truth, he will guide you to all truth. He will not speak on his own, but he will speak what he hears, and will declare to you the things that are coming. He will glorify me, because he will take from what is mine and declare it to you. Everything that the Father has is mine; for this reason I told you that he will take from what is mine and declare it to you." JOHN 16:7–15

He delivered us from the power of darkness and transferred us to the kingdom of his beloved Son, in whom we have redemption, the forgiveness of sins.
COLOSSIANS 1:13–14

For the Son of God, Jesus Christ, who was proclaimed to you by us, Silvanus and Timothy and me, was not "yes" and "no", but "yes" has been in him. For however many are the promises of God, their Yes is in him; therefore, the Amen from us also goes through him to God for glory. But the one who gives us security with you in Christ and who anointed us is God; . . . 2 CORINTHIANS 1:19–21

Therefore, since we have such hope, we act very boldly and not like Moses, who put a veil over his face so that the Israelites could not look intently at the cessation of what was fading. Rather, their thoughts were rendered dull, for to this present day the same veil remains uplifted when they read the old covenant, because through Christ it is taken away. To this day, in fact, whenever Moses is read, a veil lies over their hearts, but whenever a person turns to the Lord the veil is removed. 2 CORINTHIANS 3:12–16

Moreover, God is able to make every grace abundant for you, so that in all things, always having all you need, you may have an abundance for every good work. As it is written:
"He scatters abroad, he gives to the poor;

his righteousness endures forever."

The one who supplies seed to the sower and bread for food will supply and multiply your seed and increase the harvest of your righteousness.

2 CORINTHIANS 9:8–10

You are being enriched in every way for all generosity, which through us produces thanksgiving to God, for the administration of this public service is not only supplying the needs of the holy ones but is also overflowing in many acts of thanksgiving to God. Through the evidence of this service, you are glorifying God for your obedient confession of the gospel of Christ and the generosity of your contribution to them and to all others, while in prayer on your behalf they long for you, because of the surpassing grace of God upon you. Thanks be to God for his indescribable gift!

2 CORINTHIANS 9:11–15

Before faith came, we were held in custody under law, confined for the faith that was to be revealed. Consequently, the law was our disciplinarian for Christ, that we might be justified by faith. But now that faith has come, we are no longer under a disciplinarian. For through faith you are all children of God in Christ Jesus. For all of you who were baptized into Christ have clothed yourselves with Christ. There is neither Jew nor Greek, there is neither slave nor free person, there is not male and female; for you are all one in Christ Jesus. And if you belong to Christ, then you are Abraham's descendants, heirs according to the promise. GALATIANS 3:23–29

But when the fullness of time had come, God sent his Son, born of a woman, born under the law, to ransom those under the law, so that we might receive adoption. As proof that you are children, God sent the spirit of his Son into our hearts, crying out, 'Abba, Father!" So you are no longer a slave but a child, and if a child then also an heir, through God.

GALATIANS 4:4–7

In contrast, the fruit of the Spirit is love, joy, peace, patience, kindness, generosity, faithfulness, gentleness, self-control. Against such there is no law. Now those who belong to Christ [Jesus] have crucified their flesh with its passions and desires.

GALATIANS 5:22–24

I know indeed how to live in humble circumstances; I know also how to live with abundance. In every circumstance and in all things I have learned the secret of being well fed and of going hungry, of living in abundance and of being in need. I have the strength for everything through him who empowers me.

PHILIPPIANS 4:12–13

Blessed be the God and Father of our Lord Jesus Christ, who has blessed us in Christ with every spiritual blessing in the heavens, as he chose us in him before the foundation of the world, to be holy and without blemish before him. In love he destined us for adoption to himself through Jesus Christ, in accord with the favour of his will, for the praise of the glory of his grace that he granted us in the beloved.

EPHESIANS 1:3–6

In him we have redemption by his blood, the forgiveness of transgressions, in accord with the riches of his grace that he lavished upon us. In all wisdom and insight, he has made known to us the mystery of his will in accord with his favour that he set forth in him as a plan for the fullness of times, to sum up all things in Christ, in heaven and on earth.

EPHESIANS 1:7–10

But God, who is rich in mercy, because of the great love he had for us, even when we were dead in our transgressions, brought us to life with Christ (by grace you have been saved), raised us up with him, and seated us with him in the heavens in Christ Jesus, that in the ages to come he might show the immeasurable riches of his grace in his kindness to us in Christ Jesus. For by grace you have been saved through faith, and this is not from you; it is the gift of God; it is not from works, so no one may boast. For we are his handiwork, created in Christ Jesus for the good works that God has prepared in advance, that we should live in them. EPHESIANS 2:4–10

Therefore, remember that at one time you, Gentiles in the flesh, called the uncircumcision by those called the circumcision, which is done in the flesh by human hands, were at that time without Christ, alienated from the community of Israel and strangers to the covenants of promise, without hope and without God in the world. But now in Christ Jesus you who once were far off have become near by the blood of Christ. EPHESIANS 2:11–13

"What eye has not seen, and ear has not heard,
and what has not entered the human heart,
what God has prepared for those who love him,"
this God has revealed to us through the Spirit.

For the Spirit scrutinizes everything, even the depths of God. Among human beings, who knows what pertains to a person except the spirit of the person that is within? Similarly, no one knows what pertains to God except the Spirit of God. We have not received the spirit of the world but the Spirit that is from God, so that we may understand the things freely given us by God. And we speak about them not with words taught by human wisdom, but with words taught by the Spirit, describing spiritual realities in spiritual terms. 1 CORINTHIANS 2:9b–13

In him we were also chosen, destined to accord with the purpose of the One who accomplishes all things according to the intention of his will, so that we might exist for the praise of his glory, we who first hoped in Christ. In him you also, who have heard the word of truth, the gospel of your salvation, and have believed in him, were sealed with the promised holy Spirit, which is the first installment of our inheritance toward redemption as God's possession, to the praise of his glory. EPHESIANS 1:11–14

Turning to the disciples in private he said, "Blessed are the eyes that see what you see. For I say to you, many prophets and kings desired to see what you see, but did not see it, and to hear what you hear, but did not hear it." LUKE 10:23–24

"Do not be afraid any longer, little flock, for your Father is pleased to give you the kingdom."

LUKE 12:32

And the Word became flesh
   and made his dwelling among us,
   and we saw his glory,
   the glory as of the Father's only Son,
   full of grace and truth.
John testified to him and cried out, saying, "This was he of whom I said, 'The one who is coming after me ranks ahead of me because he existed before me.'" From his fullness we have all received, grace in place of grace, because while the law was given through Moses, grace and truth came through Jesus Christ. No one has ever seen God. The only Son, God, who is at the Father's side, has revealed him.

JOHN 1:14-18

For God so loved the world that he gave his only Son, so that everyone who believes in him might not perish but might have eternal life. For God did not send his Son into the world to condemn the world, but that the world might be saved through him. Whoever believes in him will not be condemned, but whoever does not believe has already been condemned, because he has not believed in the name of the only Son of God. JOHN 3:16-18

20

The Church's Witness to the World

In days to come,
the mountain of the LORD's house
   shall be established as the highest mountain
   and raised above the hills.
All nations shall stream towards it;
   many peoples shall come and say:
"Come, let us climb the LORD's mountain,
   to the house of the God of Jacob,
That he may instruct us in his ways,
   and we may walk in his paths."
For from Zion shall go forth instruction,
   and the word of the LORD from Jerusalem.
                      ISAIAH 2:2–3

Do everything without grumbling or questioning, that you may be blameless and innocent, children of God without blemish in the midst of a crooked and perverse generation, among whom you shine like lights in the world, as you hold on to the word of life, so that my boast for the day of Christ may be that I did not run in vain or labour in vain. PHILIPPIANS 2:14–16

"You are the salt of the earth. But if salt loses its taste, with what can it be seasoned? It is no longer good for anything but to be thrown out and trampled underfoot. You are the light of the world. A city set on a mountain cannot be hidden. Nor do they light a lamp and then put it under a bushel basket; it is set on a lampstand, where it gives light to all in the house. Just so, your light must shine before others, that they may see your good deeds and glorify your heavenly Father." MATTHEW 5:13–16

I, the LORD, have called you for the victory of
    justice,
  I have grasped you by the hand;
I formed you, and set you
  as a covenant of the people,
  a light for the nations,
To open the eyes of the blind,
  to bring out prisoners from confinement,
  and from the dungeon, those who live in darkness.
                                        ISAIAH 42:6–7

Then Jesus approached and said to them, "All power in heaven and earth has been given to me. Go, therefore, and make disciples of all nations, baptizing them in the name of the Father, and of the Son, and of the holy Spirit, teaching them to observe all that I have commanded you. And behold, I am with you always, until the end of the age." MATTHEW 28:18–20

"But you will receive power when the holy Spirit comes upon you, and you will be my witnesses in Jerusalem, throughout Judea and Samaria, and to the ends of the earth." ACTS 1:8

Now when they heard this, they were cut to the heart, and they asked Peter and the other apostles, "What are we to do, my brothers?" Peter [said] to them, "Repent and be baptized, every one of you, in the name of Jesus Christ for the forgiveness of your sins; and you will receive the gift of the holy Spirit. For the promise is made to you and to your children and to all those far off, whomever the Lord our God will call.' Acts 2:37–39

"When the Advocate comes whom I will send you from the Father, the Spirit of truth that proceeds from the Father, he will testify to me. And you also testify because you have been with me from the beginning." John 15:26–27

Let us not grow tired of doing good, for in the due time we shall reap our harvest, if we do not give up. So then, while we have the opportunity, let us do good to all, but especially to those who belong to the family of the faith. Galatians 6:9–10

"Whoever receives you receives me, and whoever receives me receives the one who sent me. Whoever receives a prophet because he is a prophet will receive a prophet's reward, and whoever receives a righteous man because he is righteous will receive a righteous man's reward. And whoever gives only a cup of cold water to one of these little ones to drink because he is a disciple – amen, I say to you, he will surely not lose his reward." Matthew 10:40–42

Jesus summoned them and said to them, "You know that those who are recognized as rulers over the Gentiles lord it over them, and their great ones make their authority over them felt. But it shall not be so among you. Rather, whoever wishes to be great among you will be your servant; whoever wishes to be first among you will be the slave of all. For the Son of Man did not come to be served but to serve and to give his life as a ransom for many." MARK 10:42–45

He said to them, "Go into the whole world and proclaim the gospel to every creature. Whoever believes and is baptized will be saved; whoever does not believe will be condemned. These signs will accompany those who believe; in my name they will drive out demons, they will speak new languages. They will pick up serpents [with their hands], and if they drink any deadly thing, it will not harm them. They will lay hands on the sick, and they will recover." MARK 16:15–18

21

Consolation in Persecution

"My children, bear patiently the anger
  that has come from God upon you.
Your enemies have persecuted you,
  and you will soon see their destruction
  and trample upon their necks." BARUCH 4:25

Say not, "I will repay evil!"
  Trust in the LORD and he will help you.

PROVERBS 20:22

"But I say to you, love your enemies, and pray for
those who persecute you, that you may be children of
your heavenly Father, for he makes his sun rise on the
bad and the good, and causes rain to fall on the just
and the unjust. For if you love those who love you,
what recompense will you have? Do not the tax
collectors do the same? And if you greet your brothers
only, what is unusual about that? Do not the pagans
do the same? So be perfect, just as your heavenly
Father is perfect." MATTHEW 5:44—48

"Blessed are they who are persecuted for
  the sake of righteousness,
for theirs is the kingdom of heaven.
Blessed are you when they insult you and persecute

you and utter every kind of evil against you [falsely] because of me. Rejoice and be glad, for your reward will be great in heaven. Thus they persecuted the prophets who were before you." MATTHEW 5:10–12

"And do not be afraid of those who kill the body but cannot kill the soul; rather, be afraid of the one who can destroy both soul and body in Gehenna. Are not two sparrows sold for a small coin? Yet not one of them falls to the ground without your Father's knowledge. Even all the hairs of your head are counted."
MATTHEW 10:28–30

Beloved, do not be surprised that a trial by fire is occurring among you, as if something strange were happening to you. But rejoice to the extent that you share in the sufferings of Christ, so that when his glory is revealed you may also rejoice exultantly. If you are insulted for the name of Christ, blessed are you, for the Spirit of glory and of God rests upon you. 1 PETER 4:12–14

"If the world hates you, realize that it hated me first. If you belonged to the world, the world would love its own; but because you do not belong to the world, and I have chosen you out of the world, the world hates you. Remember the word I spoke to you, "No slave is greater than his master." If they persecuted me, they will also persecute you. If they kept my word, they will also keep yours. And they will do all these things to you on account of my name, because they do not know the one who sent me."
JOHN 15:18–21

We are afflicted in every way, but not constrained; perplexed, but not driven to despair; persecuted, but not abandoned, struck down, but not destroyed; always carrying about in the body the dying of Jesus, so that the life of Jesus may also be manifested in our body. For we who live are constantly being given up to death for the sake of Jesus, so that the life of Jesus may be manifested in our mortal flesh . . .

Therfore, we are not discouraged; rather, although our outer self is wasting away, our inner self is being renewed day by day. For this momentary light affliction is producing for us an eternal weight of glory beyond all comparison, as we look not to what is seen but to what is unseen; for what is seen is transitory, but what is unseen is eternal. 2 CORINTHIANS 4:8–11, 16–18

For to you has been granted, for the sake of Christ, not only to believe in him but also to suffer for him. Yours is the same struggle as you saw in me and now hear about me. PHILIPPIANS 1:29–30

"I have told you this so that you may not fall away. They will expel you from the synagogues; in fact, the hour is coming when everyone who kills you will think he is offering worship to God. They will do this because they have not known either the Father or me. I have told you this so that when their hour comes you may remember that I told you." JOHN 16:1–4

"Behold, I am sending you like sheep in the midst of wolves; so be shrewd as serpents and simple as doves. But beware of people, for they will hand you over to courts and scourge you in their synagogues, and you will be led before governors and kings for my sake as a witness before them and the pagans. When they hand you over, do not worry about how you are to speak or what you are to say. You will be given at that moment what you are to say. For it will not be you who speak but the Spirit of your Father speaking through you.

"Brother will hand over brother to death, and the father his child; children will rise up against parents and have them put to death. You will be hated by all because of my name, but whoever endures to the end will be saved. When they persecute you in one town, flee to another. Amen, I say to you, you will not finish the towns of Israel before the Son of Man comes."

MATTHEW 10:16–23

"Therefore do not be afraid of them. Nothing is concealed that will not be revealed, nor secret that will not be known. What I say to you in the darkness, speak in the light; what you hear whispered, proclaim on the housetops. And do not be afraid of those who kill the body but cannot kill the soul; rather, be afraid of the one who can destroy both soul and body in Gehenna. Are not two sparrows sold for a small coin? Yet not one of them falls to the ground without your Father's knowledge. Even all the hairs of your head are counted. So do not be afraid; you are worth more than many sparrows. Everyone who acknowledges me before others I will acknowledge before my heavenly Father. But whoever denies me before others, I will deny before my heavenly Father." MATTHEW 10:26–33

Join with others in being imitators of me, brothers, and observe those who thus conduct themselves according to the model you have in us. For many, as I have often told you and now tell you even in tears, conduct themselves as enemies of the cross of Christ. Their end is destruction. Their God is their stomach; their glory is in their "shame". Their minds are occupied with earthly things. But our citizenship is in heaven, and from it we also await a saviour, the Lord Jesus Christ. He will change our lowly body to conform with his glorified body by the power that enables him also to bring all things into subjection to himself. PHILIPPIANS 3:17–21

"Then they will hand you over to persecution, and they will kill you. You will be hated by all nations because of my name. And then many will be led into sin; they will betray and hate one another. Many false prophets will arise and deceive many; and because of the increase of evildoing, the love of many will grow cold. But the one who perseveres to the end will be saved. And this gospel of the kingdom will be preached throughout the world as a witness to all nations, and then the end will come."

MATTHEW 24:9–14

"Watch out for yourselves. They will hand you over to the courts. You will be beaten in synagogues. You will be arraigned before governors and kings because of me, as a witness before them. But the gospel must first be preached to all nations. When they lead you away and hand you over, do not worry beforehand about what you are to say. But say whatever will be given to you at that hour. For it will not be you who are speaking but the holy Spirit. Brother will hand over brother to death, and the father his child; children will rise up against parents and have them put to death. You will be hated by all because of my name. But the one who perseveres to the end will be saved." MARK 13:9–13

"Before all this happens, however, they will seize and persecute you, they will hand you over to the synagogues and to prisons, and they will have you led before kings and governors because of my name. It will lead to your giving testimony. Remember, you are not to prepare your defence beforehand, for I myself shall give you a wisdom in speaking that all your adversaries will be powerless to resist or refute. You will even be handed over by parents, brothers, relatives, and friends, and they will put some of you to death. You will be hated by all because of my name, but not a hair on your head will be destroyed. By your perseverance you will secure your lives."

LUKE 21:12–19

"Amen, amen, I say to you, you will weep and mourn, while the world rejoices; you will grieve, but your grief will become joy. When a woman is in labour, she is in anguish because her hour has arrived; but when she has given birth to a child, she no longer remembers the pain because of her joy that a child has been born into the world. So you also are now in anguish. But I will see you again, and your hearts will rejoice, and no one will take your joy away from you."

JOHN 16:20–22

"But to you who hear I say, love your enemies, do good to those who hate you, bless those who curse you, pray for those who mistreat you. To the person who strikes you on one cheek, offer the other one as well, and from the person who takes your cloak, do not withhold even your tunic. Give to everyone who asks of you, and from the one who takes what is yours do not demand it back. Do to others as you would have them do to you. For if you love those who love you, what credit is that to you? Even sinners love those who love them. And if you do good to those who do good to you, what credit is that to you? Even sinners do the same. If you lend money to those from whom you expect repayment, what credit [is] that to you? Even sinners lend to sinners, and get back the same amount. But rather, love your enemies and do good to them, and lend expecting nothing back; then your reward will be great and you will be children of the Most High, for he himself is kind to the ungrateful and the wicked. Be merciful, just as [also] your Father is merciful." LUKE 6:27–36

"I gave them your word, and the world hated them, because they do not belong to the world any more than I belong to the world. I do not ask that you take them out of the world but that you keep them from the evil one. They do not belong to the world any more than I belong to the world. Consecrate them in the truth. Your word is truth. As you sent me into the world, so I sent them into the world. And I consecrate myself for them, so that they also may be consecrated in truth." JOHN 17:14–19

Remember the days past when, after you had been enlightened, you endured a great contest of suffering. At times you were publicly exposed to abuse and affliction; at other times you associated yourselves with those so treated. You even joined in the sufferings of those in prison and joyfully accepted the confiscation of your property, knowing that you had a better and lasting possession. Therefore, do not throw away your confidence; it will have great recompense. You need endurance to do the will of God and receive what he has promised. HEBREWS 10:32–36

Consider it all joy, my brothers, when you encounter various trials, for you know that the testing of your faith produces perseverance. And let perseverance be perfect, so that you may be perfect and complete, lacking in nothing. JAMES 1:2–4

Beloved, I urge you as aliens and sojourners to keep away from worldly desires that wage war against the soul. Maintain good conduct among the Gentiles, so that if they speak of you as evildoers, they may observe your good works and glorify God on the day of visitation. 1 PETER 2:11–12

Slaves, be subject to your masters with all reverence, not only to those who are good and equitable but also to those who are perverse. For whenever anyone bears the pain of unjust suffering because of consciousness of God, that is a grace. But what credit is there if you are patient when beaten for doing wrong? But if you are patient when you suffer for doing what is good, this is a grace before God. For to this you have been called, because Christ also suffered for you, leaving you an example that you should follow in his footsteps.

"He committed no sin,
    and no deceit was found in his mouth."
When he was insulted, he returned no insult; when he suffered, he did not threaten; instead, he handed himself over to the one who judges justly. He himself bore our sins in his body upon the cross, so that, free from sin, we might live for righteousness.

1 PETER 2:18–24a

Now who is going to harm you if you are enthusiastic for what is good? But even if you should suffer because of righteousness, blessed are you. Do not be afraid or terrified with fear of them, but sanctify Christ as Lord in your hearts. Always be ready to give an explanation to anyone who asks you for a reason for your hope, but do it with gentleness and reverence, keeping your conscience clear, so that, when you are maligned, those who defame your good conduct in Christ may themselves be put to shame. For it is better to suffer for doing good, if that be the will of God, than for doing evil. 1 PETER 3:13–17

But the souls of the just are in the hand of God,
    and no torment shall touch them.
They seemed, in view of the foolish, to be dead;
    and their passing away was thought an affliction
    and their going forth from us, utter destruction.
But they are in peace.

For if before men, indeed, they be punished,
  yet is their hope full of immortality;
Chastised a little, they shall be greatly blessed,
  because God tried them
  and found them worthy of himself. WISDOM 3:1–5

VI

God's Kingdom and the Fulfilment of All His Promises

22

God's Judgment of the Nations

Then shall the just one with great assurance confront
   his oppressors who set at nought his labours.
Seeing this, they shall be shaken with dreadful fear,
   and amazed at the unlooked-for salvation.
They shall say among themselves, rueful
   and groaning through anguish of spirit:
"This is he whom once we held as a laughingstock
   and as a type for mockery, fools that we were!
His life we accounted madness,
   and his death dishonoured.
See how he is accounted among the sons of God;
   how his lot is with the saints!
We, then, have strayed from the way of truth,
   and the light of justice did not shine for us,
   and the sun did not rise for us.
We had our fill of the ways of mischief and of ruin;
   we journeyed through impassable deserts,
   but the way of the LORD we knew not.
What did our pride avail us?
   what have wealth and its boastfulness afforded us?
All of them passed like a shadow
   and like a fleeting rumour;
Like a ship traversing the heaving water,
   of which, when it has passed, no trace can be
     found,
   no path of its keel in the waves." WISDOM 5:1–10

The LORD will make his glorious voice heard,
    and let it be seen how his arm descends
In raging fury and flame of consuming fire,
    in driving storm and hail. ISAIAH 30:30

Raise your eyes to the heavens,
    and look at the earth below;
Though the heavens grow thin like smoke,
    the earth wears out like a garment
    and its inhabitants die like flies,
My salvation shall remain forever
    and my justice shall never be dismayed.
Hear me, you who know justice,
    you people who have my teaching at heart:
Fear not the reproach of men,
    be not dismayed at their revilings.
They shall be like a garment eaten by moths,
    like wool consumed by grubs;
But my justice shall remain forever
    and my salvation, for all generations.
                   ISAIAH 51:6–8

The LORD has bared his holy arm
    in the sight of all the nations;
All the ends of the earth will behold
    the salvation of our God. ISAIAH 52:10

And now, O kings, give heed;
    take warning, you rulers of the earth.
Serve the LORD with fear, and rejoice before him;
    with trembling pay homage to him,
Lest he be angry and you perish from the way,
    when his anger blazes suddenly.

Happy are all who take refuge in him!
PSALM 2:10–11

For dominion is the LORD'S
  and he rules the nations.
To him alone shall bow down
  all who sleep in the earth;
Before him shall bend
  all who go down into the dust.
And to him my soul shall live; . . . PSALM 22:29–30

Men shall be abased, each one brought low,
  and the eyes of the haughty lowered,
But the LORD of hosts shall be exalted by his
    judgment,
  and God the Holy shall be shown holy by his
    justice. ISAIAH 5:15–16

I will assemble all the nations
  and bring them down to the Valley of Jehoshaphat,
And I will enter into judgment with them there
  on behalf of my people and my inheritance, Israel;
Because they have scattered them among the nations,
  and divided my land . . .
Hasten and come, all you neighbouring peoples,
  assemble there!
[Bring down, O Lord, your warriors!] JOEL 4:2, 11

Then shall you know that I, the LORD, am your God,
  dwelling on Zion, my holy mountain;
Jerusalem shall be holy,
  and strangers shall pass through her no more.
And then, on that day,

the mountains shall drip new wine,
and the hills shall flow with milk;
And the channels of Judah
shall flow with water:
A fountain shall issue from the house of the LORD,
to water the Valley of Shittim.
Egypt shall be a waste,
and Edom a desert waste,
Because of violence done to the people of Judah,
because they shed innocent blood in their land.
But Judah shall abide forever,
and Jerusalem for all generations.
I will avenge their blood,
and not leave it unpunished.
The LORD dwells in Zion. JOEL 4:17–21

Blow the trumpet in Zion,
sound the alarm on my holy mountain!
Let all who dwell in the land tremble,
for the day of the LORD is coming;
Yes, it is near, a day of darkness and of gloom,
a day of clouds and sombreness!
Like dawn spreading over the mountains,
a people numerous and mighty!
Their like has not been from of old,
nor will it be after them,
even to the years of distant generations. JOEL 2:1–2

"When the Son of Man comes in his glory, and all the angels with him, he will sit upon his glorious throne, and all the nations will be assembled before him. And he will separate them one from another, as a shepherd separates the sheep from the goats. He will place the sheep on his right hand and the goats on his left. Then the king will say to those on his right, 'Come, you who are blessed by my Father. Inherit the kingdom prepared for you from the foundation of the world. For I was hungry and you gave me food, I was thirsty and you gave me drink, a stranger and you welcomed me, naked and you clothed me, ill and you cared for me, in prison and you visited me.' Then the righteous will answer him and say, 'Lord, when did we see you hungry and feed you, or thirsty and give you drink? When did we see you a stranger and welcome you, or naked and clothe you? When did we see you ill or in prison, and visit you?' and the king will say to them in reply, 'Amen, I say to you, whatever you did for one of these least brothers of mine, you did for me.' Then he will say to those on his left, 'Depart from me, you accursed, into the eternal fire prepared for the devil and his angels. For I was hungry and you gave me no food, I was thirsty and you gave me no drink, a stranger and you gave me no welcome, naked and you gave me no clothing, ill and in prison, and you did not care for me.' Then they will answer and say, 'Lord, when did we see you, hungry or thirsty or a stranger or naked or ill or in prison, and not minister to your needs?' He will answer them, 'Amen, I say to you, what you did not do for one of these least ones, you did not do for me.' And these will go off to eternal punishment, but the righteous to eternal life." MATTHEW 25:31–46

But the LORD sits enthroned forever;
   he has set up his throne for judgment.

He judges the world with justice;
    he governs the peoples with equity. PSALM 9:8–9

The LORD is in his holy temple;
    the LORD's throne is in heaven.
His eyes behold,
    his searching glance is on mankind.
The LORD searches the just and the wicked;
    the lover of violence he hates.
He rains upon the wicked fiery coals and brimstone;
    a burning blast is their allotted cup.
For the LORD is just, he loves just deeds;
    the upright shall see his face. PSALM 11:4–7

All the ends of the earth
    Shall remember and turn to the LORD;
All the families of the nations
    shall bow down before him.
For dominion is the LORD's,
    and he rules the nations.
To him alone shall bow down
    all who sleep in the earth; . . . PSALM 22:28–31a

But God is the judge;
    one he brings low; another he lifts up.
For a cup is in the LORD's hand,
    full of spiced and foaming wine,
And he pours out from it; even to the dregs they
       shall drain it;
    all the wicked of the earth shall drink.
                      PSALM 75:8–9

God indeed will not delay,
   and like a warrior, will not be still
Till he breaks the backs of the merciless
   and wreaks vengeance upon the proud;
Till he destroys the haughty root and branch,
   and smashes the sceptre of the wicked;
Till he requites mankind according to its deeds,
   and repays men according to their thoughts;
Till he defends the cause of his people,
   and gladdens them by his mercy.
                SIRACH 35:19–23

He shall judge between the nations,
   and impose terms on many peoples.
They shall beat their swords into ploughshares
   and their spears into pruning hooks;
One nation shall not raise the sword against another,
   nor shall they train for war again. ISAIAH 2:4

. . . you will take up this taunt-song against the king
   of Babylon:
How the oppressor has reached his end!
   how the turmoil is stilled!
The LORD has broken the rod of the wicked,
   the staff of the tyrants
That struck the peoples in wrath
   Relentless blows;
That beat down the nations in anger,
   with oppression unchecked. ISAIAH 14:4–6

How have you fallen from the heavens,
   O morning star, son of the dawn!
How are you cut down to the ground,

you who mowed down the nations!
You said in your heart:
  "I will scale the heavens;
Above the stars of God
  I will set up my throne;
I will take my seat on the Mount of Assembly,
  in the recesses of the North.
I will ascend above the tops of the clouds;
  I will be like the Most High!"
Yet down to the nether world you go to the recesses
  of the pit!
When they see you they will stare,
  pondering over you:
"Is this the man who made the earth tremble,
  and kingdoms quake?
Who made the world a desert,
  razed its cities,
  and gave his captives no release?
All the kings of the nations lie in glory,
  each in his own tomb;
But you are cast forth without burial,
  loathsome and corrupt,
Clothed as those slain at sword-point,
  a trampled corpse.
Going down to the pavement of the pit,
you will never be one with them in the grave."
For you have ruined your land,
  you have slain your people!
Let him not be named forever,
  that scion of an evil race! ISAIAH 14:12–20

"Here he comes now:
  a single chariot,

a pair of horses;
He calls out and says,
    'Fallen, fallen is Babylon,
And all the images of her gods
    are smashed to the ground.'" ISAIAH 21:9

Lo, the LORD empties the land and lays it waste;
    he turns it upside down,
    scattering its inhabitants:
Layman and priest alike,
    servant and master,
The maid as her mistress,
    the buyer as the seller,
The lender as the borrower,
    the creditor as the debtor.
The earth is utterly laid waste, utterly stripped,
    for the LORD has decreed this thing.
The earth mourns and fades,
    the world languishes and fades;
    both heaven and earth languish.
The earth is polluted because of its inhabitants,
    who have transgressed laws, violated statutes,
    broken the ancient covenant. ISAIAH 24:1–5

23

God's Reward for the Just

Blessed are they who wash their robes so as to have the right to the tree of life and enter the city through its gates. REVELATION 22:14

Then shall the just one with great assurance confront
    the oppressors who set at nought his labours.
Seeing this, they shall be shaken with dreadful fear,
    and amazed at the unlooked-for salvation.
They shall say among themselves, rueful
    and groaning through anguish of spirit:
"This is he whom once we held as a laughingstock
and as a type for mockery, fools that we were!
His life we accounted madness,
    and his death dishonoured.
See how he as accounted among the sons of God;
    how his lot is with the saints!
We, then, have strayed from the way of truth,
    and the light of justice did not shine for us,
    and the sun did not rise for us." WISDOM 5:1–6

But the just live forever,
    and in the LORD is their recompense,
    and the thought of them is with the Most High.
Therefore shall they receive the splendid crown,
    The beauteous diadem, from the hand of the
    LORD –

For he shall shelter them with his right hand,
    and protect them with his arm. WISDOM 5:15–16

"Then the righteous will shine like the sun in the
kingdom of their Father. Whoever has ears ought to
hear." MATTHEW 13:43

Then the king will say to those on his right, "Come,
you who are blessed by my Father. Inherit the
kingdom prepared for you from the foundation of the
world." MATTHEW 25:34

"For the Son of Man will come with his angels in his
Father's glory, and then he will repay everyone
according to his conduct." MATTHEW 16:27

Those whom the LORD has ransomed will return
    and enter Zion singing,
    crowned with everlasting joy;
They will meet with joy and gladness,
    sorrow and mourning will flee. ISAIAH 51:11

From now on the crown of righteousness awaits me,
which the Lord, the just judge, will award to me on
that day, and not only to me, but to all who have
longed for his apperance. 2 TIMOTHY 4:8

But now they desire a better homeland, a heavenly
one. Therefore, God is not ashamed to be called their
God, for he has prepared a city for them.
                                        HEBREWS 11:16

"They will not hunger or thirst anymore,
  Nor will the sun or any heat strike them.
For the Lamb who is in the centre of the throne will
    shepherd them
    and lead them to springs of life-giving water,
    and God will wipe away every tear from their
    eyes." REVELATION 7:16–17

"For this reason they stand before God's throne
  and worship him day and night in his temple.
  The one who sits on the throne will shelter them."
                                      REVELATION 7:15

When Christ your life appears, then you too will
appear with him in glory. COLOSSIANS 3:4

But as it is written:
"What eye has not seen, and ear has not heard,
and what has not entered the human heart,
what God has prepared for those who love him," . . .
                                    1 CORINTHIANS 2:9

"He will wipe every tear from their eyes, and there
shall be no more death or mourning, wailing or pain,
[for] the old order has passed away.' REVELATION 21:4

  Blessed are they who wash their robes so as to have
the right to the tree of life and enter the city through
its gates. Outside are the dogs, the sorcerers, the
unchaste, the murderers, the idol-worshippers, and
all who love and practise deceit.
                                    REVELATION 22:14–15

On that day the LORD of hosts
   will be a glorious crown
And a brilliant diadem
   to the remnant of his people,
A spirit of justice
   to him who sits in judgment,
And strength to those
   who turn back the battle at the gate.
                          ISAIAH 28:5–6

"When the Son of Man comes in his glory, and all the angels with him, he will sit upon his glorious throne, and all the nations will be assembled before him. And he will separate them one from another, as a shepherd separates the sheep from the goats. He will place the sheep on his right and the goats on his left. Then the king will say to those on his right, 'Come, you who are blessed by my Father. Inherit the kingdom prepared for you from the foundation of the world. For I was hungry and you gave me food, I was thirsty and you gave me drink, a stranger and you welcomed me, naked and you clothed me, ill and you cared for me, in prison and you visited me.' Then the righteous will answer him and say, 'Lord, when did we see you hungry and feed you, or thirsty and give you drink? When did we see you a stranger and welcome you, or naked and clothe you? When did we see you ill or in prison, and visit you?' And the king will say to them in reply, 'Amen, I say to you, whatever you did for one of these least brothers of mine, you did for me.'" MATTHEW 25:31–40

And when the chief Shepherd is revealed, you will receive the unfading crown of glory. 1 PETER 5:4

But as for me, I know that my Vindicator lives,
  and that he will at last stand forth upon the
    dust; . . . JOB 19:25

. . . so also Christ, offered once to take away the sins
of many, will appear a second time, not to take away
sin but to bring salvation to those who eagerly await
him. HEBREWS 9:28

For the LORD is just, he loves just deeds;
  The upright shall see his face. PSALM 11:7

Yet a little while, and the wicked man shall be no
    more;
  though you mark his place he will not be there.
But the meek shall possess the land,
  they shall delight in abounding peace.
The wicked man plots against the just
  and gnashes his teeth at them; . . .
    PSALM 37:10–12

But the kindness of the LORD is from eternity
  to eternity toward those who fear him,
And his justice toward children's children
  among those who keep his covenant
  and remember to fulfill his precepts.
                    PSALMS 103:17–18

Those that sow in tears
  shall reap rejoicing.
Although they go forth weeping,
  carrying the seed to be sown,
They shall come back rejoicing,
  carrying their sheaves. PSALM 126:5–6

But the souls of the just are in the hand of God,
   and no torment shall touch them.
They seemed, in the view of the foolish, to be dead;
   and their passing away was thought an affliction
   and their going forth from us, utter destruction.
But they are in peace.
For if before men, indeed, they be punished,
   yet is their hope full of immortality;
Chastised a little, they shall be greatly blessed,
   because God tried them
   and found them worthy of himself.
As gold in the furnace, he proved them,
   and as sacrificial offerings he took them to himself.
In the time of their visitation they shall shine,
   and shall dart about as sparks through stubble;
They shall judge nations and rule over peoples,
   and the LORD shall be their King forever.
Those who trust in him shall understand truth,
   and the faithful shall abide with him in love:
Because grace and mercy are with his holy ones,
   and his care is with his elect. WISDOM 3:1–9

On that day the deaf shall hear
   the words of a book;
And out of gloom and darkness,
   the eyes of the blind shall see.
The lowly will ever find joy in the LORD,
   and the poor rejoice in the Holy One of Israel.
                  ISAIAH 29:18–19

O people of Zion, who dwell in Jerusalem,
   no more will you weep;
He will be gracious to you when you cry out,
   as soon as he hears he will answer you.

The Lord will give you the bread you need
  and the water for which you thirst.
No longer will your Teacher hide himself,
  but with your own eyes you shall see your
    Teacher,
While from behind, a voice shall sound in your ears:
  "This is the way; walk in it,"
  when you would turn to the right or to the left.

Isaiah 30:19–21

24

The Second Coming of Christ

"Behold, I am coming soon. I bring with me the recompense I will give to each according to his deeds. I am the Alpha and the Omega, the first and the last, the beginning and the end." . . .

The one who gives this testimony says, "Yes, I am coming soon." Amen! come, Lord Jesus!

REVELATION 22:12–13,20

"For the Son of Man will come with his angels in his Father's glory, and then he will repay everyone according to his conduct." MATTHEW 16:27

But as for me, I know that my Vindicator lives,
    and that he will at last stand forth upon the
        dust; . . . JOB 19:25

Behold, he is coming amid the clouds,
    and every eye will see him,
    even those who pierced him.
All the peoples of the earth will lament him.
    Yes. Amen. REVELATION 1:7

. . . so also Christ, offered once to take away the sins of many, will appear a second time, not to take away sin but to bring salvation to those who eagerly await him. HEBREWS 9:28

"Then the kingdom of heaven will be like ten virgins who took their lamps and went out to meet the bridegroom. Five of them were foolish and five were wise. The foolish ones, when taking their lamps, brought no oil with them, but the wise brought flasks of oil with their lamps. Since the bridegroom was long delayed, they all became drowsy and fell asleep. At midnight, there was a cry, "Behold, the bridegroom! Come out to meet him!" Then all those virgins got up and trimmed their lamps. The foolish ones said to the wise, 'Give us some of your oil, for our lamps are going out.' But the wise ones replied, 'No, for there may not be enough for us and you. Go instead to the merchants and buy some for yourselves.' While they went off to buy it, the bridegroom came and those who were ready went into the wedding feast with him. Then the door was locked. Afterwards the other virgins came and said, 'Lord, Lord, open the door for us!' But he said in reply, 'Amen, I say to you, I do not know you.' Therefore, stay awake, for you know neither the day nor the hour." MATTHEW 25:1–13

"There will be signs in the sun, the moon, and the stars, and on earth nations will be in dismay, perplexed by the roaring of the sea and the waves. People will die of fright in anticipation of what is coming upon the world, for the powers of the heavens will be shaken. And then they will see the Son of Man coming in a cloud with power and great glory. But when these signs begin to happen, stand erect and raise your heads because your redemption is at hand."

LUKE 21:25–28

Know this first of all, that in the last days scoffers will come [to] scoff, living according to their own desires and saying, "Where is the promise of his coming? From the time when our ancestors fell asleep, everything has remained as it was from the beginning of creation." They deliberately ignore the fact that the heavens existed of old and earth was formed out of water and through water by the word of God; through these the world that then existed was destroyed, deluged with water. The present heavens and earth have been reserved by the same word for fire, kept for the day of judgement and of destruction of the godless.

But do not ignore this one fact, beloved, that with the Lord one day is like a thousand years and a thousand years like one day. The Lord does not delay his promise, as some regard "delay", but he is patient with you, not wishing that any should perish but that all should come to repentance. But the day of the Lord will come like a thief, and then the heavens will pass away with a mighty roar and the elements will be dissolved by fire, and the earth and everything done on it will be found out. 2 PETER 3:3–10

And do this because you know the time; it is the hour now for you to wake from sleep. For our salvation is nearer now than when we first believed; the night is advanced, the day is at hand. Let us then throw off the works of darkness [and] put on the armour of light; let us conduct ourselves properly as in the day, not in orgies and drunkenness, not in promiscuity and licentiousness, not in rivalry and jealousy. But put on the Lord Jesus Christ, and make no provision for the desires of the flesh.

ROMANS 13:11–14

"Beware that your hearts do not become drowsy from carousing and drunkenness and the anxieties of daily life, and that day catch you by surprise like a trap. For that day will assault everyone who lives on the face of the earth. Be vigilant at all times and pray that you have the strength to escape the tribulations that are imminent and to stand before the Son of Man." LUKE 21:34–36

For the Lord himself, with a word of command, with the voice of an archangel and with the trumpet of God, will come down from heaven, and the dead in Christ will rise first. Then we who are alive, who are left, will be caught up together with them in the clouds to meet the Lord in the air. Thus we shall always be with the Lord. Therefore, console one another with these words. THESSALONIANS 4:16–18

From now on the crown of righteousness awaits me, which the Lord, the just judge, will award me on that day, and not only to me, but to all who have longed for his appearance. 2 TIMOTHY 4–8

"And then the sign of the Son of Man will appear in heaven, and all the tribes of the earth will mourn, and they will see the Son of Man coming upon the clouds of heaven with power and great glory. And he will send out his angels with a trumpet blast, and they will gather his elect from the four winds, from one end of the heavens to the other." MATTHEW 24:30–31

"But of that day and hour no one knows, neither the angels of heaven, nor the Son, but the Father alone. For as it was in the days of Noah, so it will be at the coming of the Son of Man. In [those] days before the flood, they were eating and drinking, marrying and giving in marriage, up to the day that Noah entered the ark. They did not know until the flood came and carried them all away. So will it be [also] at the coming of the Son of Man. Two men will be out in the field; one will be taken, and one will be left. Two women will be grinding at the mill; one will be taken, and one will be left. Therefore, stay awake! For you do not know on which day your Lord will come. Be sure of this: if the master of the house had known the hour of night when the thief was coming, he would have stayed awake and not let his house be broken into. So too, you also must be prepared, for at an hour you do not expect, the Son of Man will come." MATTHEW 24:36–44

Then Jesus answered, "I am;
and you will see the Son of Man
   seated at the right hand of the Power
   and coming with the clouds of heaven."
                     MARK 14:62

They said, "Men of Galilee, why are you standing there looking at the sky? This Jesus who has been taken up from you into heaven will return in the same way as you have seen him going into heaven."

ACTS 1:11

. . . and that the Lord may grant you times of refreshment and send you the Messiah already appointed for you, Jesus, whom heaven must receive until the times of universal restoration of which God spoke through the mouth of his holy prophets from of old. ACTS 3:20–21

"You heard me tell you, 'I am going away and I will come back to you.' If you loved me, you would rejoice that I am going to the Father; for the Father is greater than I." JOHN 14:28

That day his feet shall rest upon the Mount of Olives which is opposite Jerusalem to the east. The Mount of Olives shall be cleft in two from east to west by a very deep valley, and half of the mountain shall move to the north and half of it to the south.

ZECHARIAH 14:4

"Blessed are those servants whom the master finds vigilant on his arrival. Amen, I say to you, he will gird himself, have them recline at table, and proceed to wait on them." LUKE 12:37

25

God's Everlasting Reign in Glory

For this momentary light affliction is producing for us an eternal weight of glory beyond all comparison, as we look not to what is seen but to what is unseen; for what is seen is transitory, but what is unseen is eternal. 2 CORINTHIANS 4:17–18

No longer shall the sun
   be your light by day,
Nor the brightness of the moon
   shine upon you at night;
The LORD shall be your light forever,
   your God shall be your glory. ISAIAH 60:19

"He will wipe every tear from their eyes, and there shall be no more death or mourning, wailing or pain, [for] the old order has passed away."

REVELATION 21:4

Night will be no more, nor will they need light from lamp or sun, for the Lord God shall give them light and they shall reign forever and ever.

REVELATION 22:5

I saw no temple in the city, for its temple is the Lord God almighty and the Lamb. The city had no need of sun or moon to shine on it, for the glory of

God gave it light, and its lamp was the Lamb. The nations will walk by its light, and to it the kings of the earth will bring their treasure. During the day its gates will never be shut, and there will be no night there. REVELATION 21:22–25

"For this reason they stand before God's throne
    and worship him day and night in his temple.
    The one who sits on the throne will shelter them.
They will not hunger or thirst anymore,
    nor will the sun or any heat strike them.
For the Lamb who is in the centre of the throne will shepherd them
    and lead them to springs of life-giving water,
    and God will wipe away every tear from their eyes." REVELATION 7:15–17

When Christ your life appears, then you too will appear with him in glory. COLOSSIANS 3:4

. . . who will repay everyone according to his works: eternal life to those who seek glory, honour, and immortality through perseverance in good works, . . . ROMANS 2:6–7

But rejoice to the extent that you share in the sufferings of Christ, so that when his glory is revealed you may also rejoice exultantly. 1 Peter 4:13

. . . and if children, then heirs, heirs of God and joint heirs of Christ, if only we suffer with him so that we may also be glorified with him.

I consider that the sufferings of this present time

are as nothing compared with the glory to be revealed
for us. ROMANS 8:17–18

Only goodness and kindness follow me
    all the days of my life;
And I shall dwell in the house of the LORD
    for years to come. PSALM 23:6

But our citizenship is in heaven, and from it we also
await a saviour, the Lord Jesus Christ. He will change
our lowly body to conform with his glorified body by
the power that enables him also to bring all things
into subjection to himself. PHILIPPIANS 3:20–21

Beloved, we are God's children now; what we shall be
has not yet been revealed. We do know that when it is
revealed we shall be like him, for we shall see him as
he is. I John 3:2

. . . "that you may eat and drink at my table in my
kingdom; and you will sit on thrones judging the
twelve tribes of Israel." LUKE 22:30

Blessed be the God and Father of our Lord Jesus
Christ, who in his great mercy gave us a new birth to
a living hope through the resurrection of Jesus Christ
from the dead, to an inheritance that is imperishable,
undefiled, and unfading, kept in heaven for you . . .
                                1 PETER 1:3–4

Nations shall behold your vindication,
    and all kings your glory;
You shall be called by a new name

pronounced by the mouth of the LORD.
You shall be a glorious crown in the hand of the
     LORD,
   a royal diadem held by your God. ISAIAH 62:2–3

. . . as a plan for the fullness of times, to sum up all
things in Christ, in heaven and earth . . . And he put
all things beneath his feet and gave him as head over
all things to the church, which is his body, the fullness
of the one who fills all things in every way.
                                        EPHESIANS 1:10, 22–23

"Zion is my resting place forever;
   in her will I dwell, for I prefer her.
I will bless her with abundant provision,
   her poor I will fill with bread.
Her priests I will clothe with salvation,
   and her faithful ones shall shout merrily for joy.
In her will I make a horn to sprout forth for David;
   I will place a lamp for my anointed.
His enemies I will clothe with shame,
   but upon him my crown shall shine."
                                        PSALM 132:14–18

   On that day,
The branch of the LORD will be lustre and glory,
   and the fruit of the earth will be honour and
      splendour for the survivors of Israel.
He who remains in Zion
   and he that is left in Jerusalem
Will be called holy:
   every one marked down for life in Jerusalem.
When the Lord washes away

the filth of the daughters of Zion,
And purges Jerusalem's blood from her midst
    with a blast of searing judgment,
Then will the LORD create,
    over the whole site of Mount Zion
    and over her place of assembly,
A smoking cloud by day
    and a light of flaming fire by night.
For over all, his glory will be shelter and protection:
    shade from the parching heat of day,
    refuge and cover from storm and rain.
                    ISAIAH 4:2–6

With joy you will draw water
    at the fountain of salvation, and say on that day:
Give thanks to the LORD, acclaim his name;
    among the nations make known his deeds,
    proclaim how exalted is his name.
Sing praise to the LORD for his glorious achievement;
    let this be known throughout all the earth.
Shout with exultation, O city of Zion,
    for great in your midst
    is the Holy One of Israel! ISAIAH 12:3–6

On this mountain the LORD of hosts
    will provide for all peoples
A feast of rich food and choice wines,
    juicy, rich food and pure, choice wines.
On this mountain he will destroy
    the veil that veils all peoples,
The web that is woven over all nations;
    he will destroy death forever.
The Lord God will wipe away

201

the tears from all faces;
The reproach of his people he will remove
   from the whole earth; for the LORD has spoken.
      On that day it will be said:
"Behold our God, to whom we looked to save us!
   This is the LORD for whom we looked;
      let us rejoice and be glad that he has saved us!"
                    ISAIAH 25:6–9

The light of the moon will be like that of the sun
   and the light of the sun will be seven times greater
   [like the light of seven days].
On the day the LORD binds up the wounds of his
     people,
   he will heal the bruises left by his blows.
                    ISAIAH 30:26

Your eyes will see a king in his splendour,
   they will look upon a vast land . . .
Look to Zion, the city of our festivals;
   let your eyes see Jerusalem
   as a quiet abode, a tent not to be struck,
Whose pegs will never be pulled up,
   nor any of its ropes severed.
Indeed the LORD will be there with us, majestic;
   yes, the LORD our judge, the LORD our lawgiver,
   the LORD our king, he it is who will save us.
                ISAIAH 33:17, 20, 22

The desert and the parched land will exult;
   the steppe will rejoice and bloom.
They will bloom with abundant flowers,
   And rejoice with joyful song . . .

God's Everlasting Reign in Glory

Those whom the LORD has ransomed will return
 and enter Zion singing,
  crowned with everlasting joy;
They will meet with joy and gladness,
 sorrow and mourning will flee. ISAIAH 35:1–2, 10

Also available in Fount Paperbacks

A Gift for God
MOTHER TERESA OF CALCUTTA

'The force of her words is very great . . . the message is always the same, yet always fresh and striking.'

Malcolm Muggeridge

Strength to Love
MARTIN LUTHER KING

'The sermons . . . read easily and reveal a man of great purpose, humility and wisdom . . . in the turbulent context of the American race conflict, Dr King's statements have the ring of social as well as spiritual truth . . .'

Steven Kroll
The Listener

A Book of Comfort
ELIZABETH GOUDGE

'The contents are worth ten of the title: this is a careful, sensitive anthology of the illuminations in prose and verse that have prevented the world from going wholly dark over the centuries.'

Sunday Times

The Desert in the City
CARLO CARRETTO

'. . . we have been in the hands of one of the finest of modern spiritual writers, who helps us on the road of love in Christ.'

Philip Cauvin, the Universe

Also available in Fount Paperbacks

Mother Teresa: Her People and Her Work
DESMOND DOIG

'Desmond Doig has written a beautiful book and his writing and the pictures capture Mother Teresa and her people and her work exactly. He understands it. I want to cry, with anger, with passion, with compassion, with sadness at the waste of human life and energy. But no, that is not enough, it is a waste of energy, we must do something to help her.'

Financial Times

Something Beautiful for God
MALCOLM MUGGERIDGE

'For me, Mother Teresa of Calcutta embodies Christian love in action. Her face shines with the love of Christ on which her whole life is centred. *Something Beautiful for God* is about her and the religious order she has instituted.'

Malcolm Muggeridge

A Gift for God
MOTHER TERESA

'This selection of Mother Teresa's sayings, prayers, meditations, letters and addresses on themes of love and compassion . . . touches profound spiritual themes . . . Its size belies its power to inspire and uplift.'

Church of England Newspaper

The Love of Christ
MOTHER TERESA

A further collection of Mother Teresa's writings and sayings, including hitherto unpublished extracts from her retreat addresses to her community of nuns.

'Do not read this book . . . if you do not want . . . to be shaken in conscience and shamed into loving God and other people more.'

Iain Mackenzie, Church Times

Also available in Fount Paperbacks

Jesus – The Man Who Lives
MALCOLM MUGGERIDGE

'This book is excellently produced and beautifully illustrated
. . . it bears witness to Malcolm Muggeridge's deep convictions,
his devotion to the person of Jesus.'
Mervyn Stockwood, Church of England Newspaper

Jesus Rediscovered
MALCOLM MUGGERIDGE

'. . . one of the most beautifully written, perverse, infuriating,
enjoyable and moving books of the year.'
David Edwards, Church Times

Mister Jones, Meet the Master
PETER MARSHALL

'Here is a book of sermons like nothing else on earth . . .
forthright, easily understood and intensely human . . .'
Hector Harrison, NSW Presbyterian

Also available in Fount Paperbacks

BOOKS BY C. S. LEWIS

Reflections on the Psalms

'Absolutely packed with wisdom. It is clearly the fruit of very much reflection . . . upon one's own darkness of spirit, one's own fumbling and grasping in the shadows of prayer or of penitence.'

Trevor Huddleston

Miracles

'This is a brilliant book, abounding in lucid exposition and illuminating metaphor.'

Charles Davey, The Observer

The Problem of Pain

'Written with clarity and force, and out of much knowledge and experience.'

Times Literary Supplement

Surprised by Joy

'His outstanding gift is clarity. You can take it at two levels, as straight autobiography, or as a kind of spiritual thriller, a detective's probing of clue and motive . . .'

Isabel Quigley, Sunday Times

Fount Paperbacks

Fount is one of the leading paperback publishers of religious books and below are some of its recent titles.

- ☐ FRIENDSHIP WITH GOD David Hope £2.95
- ☐ THE DARK FACE OF REALITY Martin Israel £2.95
- ☐ LIVING WITH CONTRADICTION Esther de Waal £2.95
- ☐ FROM EAST TO WEST Brigid Marlin £3.95
- ☐ GUIDE TO THE HERE AND HEREAFTER
  Lionel Blue/Jonathan Magonet £4.50
- ☐ CHRISTIAN ENGLAND (1 Vol) David Edwards £10.95
- ☐ MASTERING SADHANA Carlos Valles £3.95
- ☐ THE GREAT GOD ROBBERY George Carey £2.95
- ☐ CALLED TO ACTION Fran Beckett £2.95
- ☐ TENSIONS Harry Williams £2.50
- ☐ CONVERSION Malcolm Muggeridge £2.95
- ☐ INVISIBLE NETWORK Frank Wright £2.95
- ☐ THE DANCE OF LOVE Stephen Verney £3.95
- ☐ THANK YOU, PADRE Joan Clifford £2.50
- ☐ LIGHT AND LIFE Grazyna Sikorska £2.95
- ☐ CELEBRATION Margaret Spufford £2.95
- ☐ GOODNIGHT LORD Georgette Butcher £2.95
- ☐ GROWING OLDER Una Kroll £2.95

All Fount Paperbacks are available at your bookshop or newsagent, or they can be ordered by post from Fount Paperbacks, Cash Sales Department, G.P.O. Box 29, Douglas, Isle of Man. Please send purchase price plus 22p per book, maximum postage £3. Customers outside the UK send purchase price, plus 22p per book. Cheque, postal order or money order. No currency.

NAME (Block letters) _____

ADDRESS_____

_____

_____